# SHOW ME!
## A DOG-SHOWING PRIMER

D. Caroline Coile, Ph.D.

BARRON'S

## Acknowledgments

To Baha, Tundra, Kara, Khyber, Sissy, Savannah, Hypatia, Dixie, Bobby, Kitty, Wolfman, Jeepers, Stinky, Junior, Khyzi, and Beanie, some of whom won many titles and accolades in the ring, some of whom did not, but all of whom won my heart.

© Copyright 1997 by D. Caroline Coile

All inquiries should be addressed to:
Barron's Educational Series, Inc.
250 Wireless Boulevard
Hauppauge, New York 11788

International Standard Book No. 0-8120-9710-6

Library of Congress Catalog Card No. 96-31932

**Library of Congress Cataloging-in-Publication Data**
Coile, D. Caroline.
    Show me! : a dog showing primer /
D. Caroline Coile.
        p.    cm.
    Includes bibliographical references (p.) and index.
    ISBN 0-8120-9710-6
    1. Show dogs—Handling. 2. Dogs—Showing.
3. Dog shows. I. Title.
SF425.C64    1997
636.7′0888—dc20                     96-31932
                                               CIP

Printed in China

987

## About the Author

Caroline Coile is an award-winning author who has been showing dogs since 1974. Her "Baha" salukis (named in honor of her first saluki, Baha) have been top ranked in conformation, obedience, and field competition, and include Best in Show, Best in Specialty, and Best in Field winners, all owner-handled. In 1995 Caroline was awarded the American Saluki Association distinction of "Handler of the Year," and one of her salukis, "Dog of the Year."

The author's interest in dogs shaped her educational goals, where her curiosity about canine behavior and genetics ultimately led to a Ph.D. in the area of biopsychology/neuroscience, with special expertise in canine sensory systems.

## Photo Credits

Margarita Agramonte: pages 46, 47, 49; Alverson Photographers: page 120; John Ashbey: pages 36, 37; Barbara Augello: inside front cover; Rich Bergman: page 53; Jane Bishop: pages 1, 38, 50, 51; Paulette Braun: back cover, pages 5, 9, 24, 57, 68 top, 83, 106, 107, 110, 111, 113; Caroline Coile: pages viii, 41, 45, 52, 69, 66, 121, 122; Warren Cook: page 55; Gay Glazbrook: front cover, pages 22, 44, 75 bottom, 80, 112; Susan Green: inside back cover; Dale Jackson: pages 21, 91, 108; Michael Ross: pages 4, 8, 12, 14 bottom, 15, 48, 56, 65, 71, 72, 75 top, 84, 119, 118, 125; Pam Ross: page 68 bottom; Bob Schwartz: pages 3, 35, 90, 102, 103, 104, 105, 123, 137; Leslie Simis: pages 10, 13, 14 top, 18, 74, 76, 85, 109, 115, 116, 117, 124, 127; Judith Strom: pages 2, 128.

## Cover Photos

Front cover: golden retriever; inside front cover: Dalmation: inside back cover: Alaksan Malamute; back cover: chow chow.

## Important Note

This book tells the reader how to show a purebred dog. The author and the publisher consider it important to point out that the advice given in the book is meant primarily for normally developed puppies from a good breeder—that is, dogs of excellent physical health and good character.

Even well-behaved and carefully supervised dogs sometimes do damage to someone else's property or cause accidents. It is therefore in the owner's interest to be adequately insured against such eventualities, and we strongly urge all dog owners to purchase a liability policy that covers their dog.

# Contents

# Preface

The other handlers seemed to know what was going on. Their dogs trotted so nicely. What was I thinking? Why had I made such a terrible mistake by entering a dog show? Why wouldn't my dog just act like the others? And now the judge was beckoning to me, apparently ordering me from the ring because my dog was so poorly trained. This was a disaster! As we attempted to leave the ring, the judge stopped us. Apparently some sort of speech on how poorly prepared we were was in order. If we could just get out of here I would *never, ever* come back to another dog show. But the judge demanded I pose my dog. Would the public humiliation never end? I grabbed desperately at my dog's feet but he wouldn't put them where I aimed them and continued to dance around. How the other exhibitors' dogs just put their feet in perfect position and stood like little statues I would never understand. Then the judge said, "Try doing it like this..." and I did, and it worked! A miracle in Ring 9! And then the judge pointed to us and said we were first place and winners dog, and someone congratulated us and said we had won a major!

So many new exhibitors experience the same frustration and bewilderment at their first attempts to show a dog, but not all are fortunate enough to find a patient judge. Unable to find out the unwritten rules of what seems like a secret society, and intimidated by experienced handlers who seem unbeatable, they take their dog and go home, never to return.

The aim of this book is to act as a mentor to the new or prospective dog exhibitor. If we learn from our mistakes, then I would surely be the most knowledgeable person in dogs, and I have tried to pass on over 20 years' worth of dog-showing mistakes through these pages. Included is information on how to find, choose, raise, and train a show dog, how to train yourself to be a good handler, and just what to expect at the dog show and in the ring. Most exhibitors lose more than they win, and ways of dealing with repeated losses are discussed. I wrote this book as the book I wish I had had by my side some 20 years ago, and I hope it catapults the neophyte over some of the hurdles that so often stop newcomers in their tracks.

You *can* beat the professional handlers. You have the advantage of being able to spend all of your time and energy preparing and working with one dog. You just need to know how to channel that work.

Of course, some things never change. There I was in the ring with my dog, a granddaughter of the one in the earlier scenario. The judge told each handler to take his or her dog to the middle of the ring and have it stand on its own. The other handlers, all professionals, seemed to know exactly what to do, baiting their dogs into perfect stances. My dog wouldn't even look at the liver I waved desperately in front of her face. My heart sank and we returned to our place in line. Then the judge seemed to be pointing in our direction. I looked to the handlers on either side of me to make sure it wasn't them the judge was pointing at, but they were congratulating me. I grabbed my dog in my arms and ran to the Best in Show marker!

*The author with one of her salukis.*

## Chapter One
# See Spot Show

Dog shows are the number one family participation sport in the country, and one of the oldest organized sports in America. The American Kennel Club sanctions over 8,000 events each year, involving tens of thousands of competing dogs. Yet dog showing is still principally a self-taught skill, and unlike any other sport, rank amateurs must compete against seasoned professionals. Disheartened by what sometimes seems a mysterious course of events and a secret pathway to success, new exhibitors who cannot find the help they need to get started, instead give up. Newcomers can compete successfully against old-timers, but they need to arrive fully prepared, with the best dog, equipment, handling savvy, and attitude available. The mission of this book is to create the best prepared newcomer possible.

## Are Dog Shows Good for Dogs?

No species has been more malleable in the hands of humans than the domestic dog. Because of the variation in size, shape, and temperament it sometimes seems hard to believe that they are all of one species. The breeds of dogs have been developed through selection over hundreds—sometimes thousands—of years to perform specific functions. The greyhound is a specialized running machine, and must have strong limbs and a supple spine, as well as the desire to chase moving objects. The border collie must be able to sprint and trot tirelessly, with a desire to intimidate and

*A champion borzoi is both beautiful and functional.*

1

*The standard of each breed describes a dog that was bred to perform a specialized task. The ideal show Labrador retriever, for example, should be built in such a way that it would be a strong swimmer with the ability to withstand cold water and the desire to bring back downed game.*

stalk sheep without attacking them. Every breed must have a specific conformation and temperament to enable it to do its job. Some breeds are still serving us in their original roles, while for others, that role has vanished. The bulldog was bred for the long outlawed sport of bull-baiting; yet, should the bulldog be allowed to become extinct simply because bull-baiting is no longer practiced? Dog shows were developed to both promote and preserve the pure breeds of dogs. The standard for each breed serves as a blueprint, and every good show dog should be able to do today the job for which it was bred hundreds of generations ago.

Not all dog breeds are ancient, and many were never expected to do more than serve as beautiful companions. These breeds are judged by no less rigorous standards, however, because, in order to be a good companion, a dog must be sound of body and mind.

Dog shows have been criticized for supposedly encouraging breeders to produce exaggerated caricatures of their breeds, sometimes along with physical deformities. Good judges, however, don't reward such exaggeration, and good breeders don't produce it. Good breeders, unlike most pet breeders, are aware of the health problems in their breed and test their stock before breeding.

Most health problems in purebred dogs are the result of naive breeding from pet owners who never heard of health problems or from puppy mill operators, who never cared.

## The Good

You will not find a show dog chained in the yard, infested with parasites, or bred every season. Show dogs receive the best veterinary care, often prompting state-of-the-art veterinary techniques. Breed clubs may fund research into a particular health problem in their breed. The American Kennel Club (AKC) funds research into the genetic problems of purebred dogs, an area that otherwise receives little financial support. All-breed clubs donate money to local humane organizations.

Dog shows encourage good sportsmanship, provide a safe and enjoyable family pastime, encourage responsible dog ownership, preserve living history in the form of dog breeds, and help to improve the health of our pets.

Some people feel sorry for show dogs because they have to get gussied up and spend the day at a dog show. True, most dogs would rather spend the day hiking, swimming, and running amok, but many dogs enjoy the opportunity to spend the day as their owner's center of attention, being groomed, praised, and admired, as well as having the chance to go for a ride, shop at the booths, and gawk at all

*The family pet can bring home the gold! (Border collie)*

the strange-looking dogs also at the show! Besides, give most people a job that requires only a couple of days a week and asks only that they run in a circle and look happy, and you'd hear few complaints.

## The Bad

With some dogs being a show dog is a full-time job, involving constant travel, daily grooming, and far too much time sitting in a cage. Coated breeds may not be allowed in the yard, to avoid getting sticks in their coat. They may be separated so that no hair is pulled out in play, or so that delicate skin does not get scratched. Black dogs may not be allowed out in sunlight, so that their coats do not get sunburned. Most breeds don't require such measures, however, and almost any dog can juggle the requirements of family pet and show dog sensation. The life of a show dog can be as good, or as bad, as you make it.

3

Everybody condemns puppy mills and backyard breeders. But too many show breeders are equally reprehensible as they breed litter after litter in search of that great puppy or a top producer award. Championships are too often considered exemption licenses from the responsibilities of overpopulation. Where do all the puppies go? The AKC estimates that 10 to 20 percent of all dogs registered come from show breeders. It is difficult to believe that there are waiting homes for all of the puppies bred. Again, dog show breeders can be as responsible or irresponsible as the rest of the world.

## Are Dog Shows Good for People?

The beauty of dog shows is that you can be involved as little, or as much, as you desire. You may wish to test the waters with a few tentative outings, or decide to plunge in and make an immediate splash. Just make sure you don't get in over your head.

### The Good

Most people get involved in showing dogs because they have a dog that is beautiful in their eyes; they are proud of their family member and want others to appreciate its gleaming qualities. Dog showing is one of the few true family sports. Everyone can be involved in preparing the dog for the ring. Dog shows can provide a destination for weekend forays, and a forum in which to meet new friends from all walks of life. They can help to foster confidence and self-esteem in young people, and provide them with a constructive weekend pastime.

Some people credit showing dogs with turning their lives around, giving them a mission in life, and supplying a wide circle of friends. The dog show community is tightknit and usually ready to lend a helping hand. Many people live from weekend to weekend, eager to rejoin their best friends at the dog show. Where else can you share the latest anecdotes about your beloved dog, the marvel of a new litter of hopefuls, and your love of a breed of dog with others who love it as well? Those who wish to leave their place in canine history can do so by improving a breed. Those who wish to help dogs can do so by becoming involved in education, research, or rescue.

## The Bad

With every silver lining there is a cloud, and the dog show world can be quite overcast. For one thing, dog showing can be expensive. Showing dogs is a luxury, a luxury sometimes undertaken by people who can barely afford life's necessities. Entry fees, gasoline, motels, show clothes, grooming equipment, food supplements, and advertising can exert a heavy toll on already stretched finances. More dogs may bring more success, but also higher food bills, veterinary bills, a need for a larger vehicle, and even a new home with a larger yard. And no exhibitors ever made money back by breeding their dogs. Lots of people make money from dog shows, but the exhibitor just spends it.

The time and work involved in becoming successful can become overwhelming. Breeds requiring extensive grooming must be groomed on schedule or risk having their coat ruined by delay. Poop must be scooped; dogs must be socialized, exercised, and trained.

If only one member of a family is bitten by the show bug, trouble can brew. The non-dog spouse can come to resent the once peaceful home being taken over by yapping dogs, money being spent on showing, and the separation during show weekends. Children may enjoy dog shows for awhile, but cannot always be expected to share their parents' interest week after week. Still, some children find weekend friends among the children of other exhibitors, and

older children can develop responsibility and a sense of pride by competing in Junior Showmanship.

**Important to bear in mind:** Because every show results in more losers than winners, the dog show exhibitor must be able to cope with losing a lot.

*Dog showing is one of the few sports in which the whole family can play a role. (ASCOB cocker spaniel)*

## Gone to the Dogs

Dog showing is strangely addicting. The addiction, if left unchecked, can ruin human and canine lives and loves. How can such an innocent family hobby go so awry? By doing it to excess.

*Overdogged* is the term used to describe someone who has acquired so many dogs that the dogs have become a hardship. It can happen before you know it. Usually the original show hopeful is discovered to not be show quality, so a show-quality dog is obtained. Then another once-in-a-lifetime dog becomes available. Perhaps this one finishes its championship, and the breeding bug bites. The dream litter arrives, but the inquiries do not. The entire litter stays. Males quarrel and have to be kept separated. The family car is too small to fit the entire crew, so a dogsitter must be hired in order to go to dog shows. The food and veterinary bills are staggering. And if one spouse was never all that crazy about the idea of going to the dogs to start with, he or she may declare an ultimatum. In some cases, divorce is the outcome. In others, the work so much overwhelms the pleasure that the dogs are dumped in animal shelters or with any takers.

Where do you keep a bunch of dogs? Attempts to keep them all in the house usually result in a house that smells like a kennel. Non-doggy friends gag as they walk in the door, and later decline to visit. No chair arm is left unchewed, no carpet unwet. At the other extreme the dogs are moved to cages in the garage, where they sit, and sit, like toys in the toy chest waiting to be taken out and played with once a week at the dog show. Otherwise, they are in the way.

## Just Say "No"

The hardest thing to learn in the dog game is the ability to say "No." No, you don't want the puppy from the sister of the dog you so admired. No, you don't want a replacement pup in addition to the first pup you got that didn't turn out. No, you don't want two pups for the price of one. No, you don't want a stud fee puppy. No, now is not the time to breed your bitch. Saying no means you will have to move more slowly in the dog game. You may not get the instant recognition that you would if you suddenly showed up with a pack of dogs. But it gives you time to learn your trade, to be ready for the next dog, and to build a solid, reliable reputation. Long-time breeders have seen the flash in the pan exhibitors come and go, the ones who start with a bang, breed a few litters, give up, and then leave the dedicated breeders to clean up after them.

Almost every breeder is over-dogged. Sometimes it can't be helped. The best reason to be over-dogged is through sentiment and love; you breed a litter, and can't place the cryptorchid male. Logic and other breeders would tell you to have it euthanized. Worthless as a show dog, it can only take up valuable space. But you caused him to come into the world and in so doing, you took the responsibility for his lifelong well-being. You love him and you promise to keep him for the rest of his life. Good for you. You love the dog—and the breed—more than the ribbons and glory. That's the true mark of a successful breeder.

## Winners and Losers

Sometimes the solution to being overdogged is worse than the problem. "He just doesn't fit into my breeding plans anymore...," "I have her daughter, so I have everything I need from her to go on...," "He's too big," "His rear is weak," "He's finished now but he's not specials quality...," "I want to breed a litter and I have too many dogs...," "He's excess baggage now that he's retired...," "He needs a home where he can get more attention..." (this latter never used with a winning dog). Each and every one of these statements has fallen upon my disbelieving ears as reasons for discarding a dog. Dog people are taught that the key to success is a ruthless attitude when it comes to disposing of dogs that are not performing up to standard. Like a poker hand, the surplus are discarded and new hopefuls take their place until they, too, have run their course. The rejects are sold, given away, or euthanized. No matter how many Best in Shows someone with this attitude wins, in my book they will always be losers.

The winners are the ones who can go home from the show ribbonless but with a true canine friend, enjoy a stroll on the beach, curl up in front of a fire, and not imagine what life could be without the best dog in the world. The winners couldn't comprehend deserting such a friend because it had cowhocks or its bite was a little off or its feet didn't travel in a straight line when it trotted. The winners know the true worth of a dog is not in the number of ribbons it can bring home, but the amount of love it gives and elicits.

If you get a dog and it doesn't turn out to meet your expectations, whose fault is that? Certainly not the dog's. It had no possible way of knowing you didn't want it to grow any bigger, or have light-colored eyes. It thought its job was to love you and be part of your family.

The typical show dog may be shown at 20 shows a year, perhaps for two years. Each outing may amount to five or ten minutes in the ring, with two minutes devoted to actually showing that dog. This amounts to about 40 shows with two minutes each, or 80 minutes of active showtime in the dog's entire life. Yet I've known people who tearfully parted with a beloved dog because it couldn't win in the ring, and often it was the human half of the team who was responsible for the losses.

When I first got involved in showing dogs, I was proud to inform people that "Yes, these are show dogs." Now I'm more proud to tell them that "No, these are just pet dogs that happen to go to shows sometimes." Sometimes people allow themselves to get carried away with a game that they got into because of their love for their dog, with the ones to ultimately pay the price being the innocent dogs who never asked to be a part of it—the poor little rich kids of the dog world.

The AKC distributes a bumper sticker with the slogan, "A dog is for life...not just for Christmas." Perhaps they need to add one for the dog-showing crowd that reads, "A dog is for life...not just for dog shows."

## Chapter Two
# Cast of Characters

## Hot Dogs

Dog shows are about dogs, and some dogs have achieved such celebrity that they are known by every dog person in the country on a first name basis. These dog stars fly from show to show, winning Best in Shows throughout the land. Some are bought or leased throughout their show careers by wealthy backers who want to help create a top winning team of dog and handler. Such dogs are usually not only good dogs, but what's more, have a certain charisma that seems to demand attention in any ring—and they get it.

*The top winning dog of all-breeds in 1995, this "haute dog" won over 50 Best in Shows and defeated almost 85,000 dogs that year. (Afghan hound)*

## Judges—Lords of the Rings

Just who are these almighty judges? They come from the ranks of former handlers and breeders. Every single one (with a few exceptions of those who were born into the sport) was once a bumbling newcomer. Unfortunately, some seem to have forgotten their humble beginnings.

Judging requires a good eye for a dog, integrity, the ability to weigh good and bad points and make decisions, and the courage of one's convictions.

To become a judge, a person must have at least ten years of experience in a breed, have bred four litters, and have finished two champions. They must have practiced by judging matches and sweepstakes, and stewarded at several shows. They must pass an interview and finally be approved by the AKC. Few new judges are granted a license to judge more than a breed or two. As they prove themselves competent, they can then apply to judge additional breeds.

Most aspiring judges have far more than the minimal requirements, and have turned to judging as the

judges fall somewhere between the two extremes. Again, judges can be good or bad, whether breeder, all-rounder, or in-between.

## Second in Command

Giving out armbands, marking dogs absent, calling the dogs into the ring, getting the proper ribbons arranged, and basically keeping everything running smoothly is the job of the *steward*. The steward has no say in judging, and must also never allow the judge to inadvertently see the catalog. (Judges are not allowed to see the names of the entries.) Stewards are usually experienced dog exhibitors who are paid a modest fee for their services.

## Ringmasters

Dog shows don't just happen. Premium lists must be mailed, entries taken, confirmations mailed, catalogs printed, tents erected, rings laid out, awards recorded, and about 1,000 questions and complaints addressed. All are handled by seasoned professionals: the dog show superintendents, whose job it is to make every dog show run as smoothly as possible. At most shows an official representative from the American Kennel Club (the "AKC rep") is present and can be located through the superintendent. The AKC rep is there to oversee the

*Good judges know that the decisions they make can affect the future of the breeds they judge, and only undertake to judge those breeds of which they have in-depth knowledge. They must be gentle with the dogs and polite and fair to the exhibitors. (Shiba inu)*

next logical step as a way to serve their breed. A few new judges have never achieved more than minimal success as breeders, and have turned to judging in an attempt to gain the admiration of others. Some judges are very good. Some are not.

You will often hear the terms *breeder-judge* and *all-rounders*. New judges are usually breeder-judges who judge only the breed of dog with which they have personal experience. A win under such a judge is considered particularly prestigious, because breeder-judges tend to know a breed in far more depth than a judge who must be familiar with 100 breeds. However, sometimes breeder-judges can get caught up on rather insignificant details and may be more influenced by the sight of all their friends on the end of the dogs' leads. All-rounders are licensed to judge all breeds of dogs, due to extensive judging experience. Most entire show, and is the person to see if a rule violation occurs.

## Hired Guns

One would think that everyone would show his or her own dog, but there are people who make a very good living handling other people's dogs. Professional handlers win more than owner handlers, mainly because they are more skilled at presenting dogs. They have been in the ring thousands of times, and have had plenty of opportunities to hone their skills and overcome their nerves. They have their choice of dogs to show, and can send a losing dog home to be replaced by a more competitive one. Judges recognize handlers, and often know them personally. Many judges are former handlers themselves, and may occasionally wish to do an old friend a favor. Other handlers have developed a reputation for showing quality dogs, and judges expect that any dog they walk into the ring with will be a fine animal.

Choosing a handler should be undertaken with almost as much research as choosing your dog. In the "old days" handlers had to be licensed by the AKC, and this provided a certain assurance that some minimum requirements had been met. Now membership in one of the professional handling organizations, such as the Professional Handler's Association (PHA), or the Dog Handler's Guild (DHG) similarly indicates

that a handler has agreed to abide by certain professional standards. Otherwise, anyone with a show lead can call himself or herself a professional handler. Not all good handlers are members of such organizations. If you need a handler, consider the following:

- Safety first. Some very skilled handlers are nonetheless irresponsible or don't have proper facilities or vehicles. If your dog is to stay with the handler, where will it be living? Can it escape or be attacked by other dogs? Is the vehicle reliable and safe? Will your dog be riding in a secure cage? Is the handler a safe driver?

*Breeds that need specialized grooming usually require handlers who specialize in that breed. Professional handlers must know the standard and the temperament of each breed they show. (Standard poodle)*

- What precautions have been taken against overheating in summer? Does the vehicle have air-conditioning? How will the dogs be kept cool when parked at the show? Is there a back up or warning system in case the power fails and the air-conditioning turns off?
- How many dogs does the handler usually travel with?
- Does the handler have an assistant who can help if there are lots of dogs?
- Is the handler overburdened or distracted by children?
- How does the handler treat dogs in his or her care? Do the dogs look happy and healthy? Are cages and facilities clean? Are dogs parasite-free?
- Does the handler make your dog look good?
- Does the handler have a good reputation and face recognition?
- How does the handler interact with competitors?
- Is the handler a good sport? As your dog's representative, you want your handler's sportsmanship to be a reflection of your own.

Make sure you understand the nature of the handling charges. In addition to the standard handling fee, there are usually fees for boarding, grooming, and training. Travel expenses are usually split by all clients sending dogs on a particular trip. Bonuses are charged for winning Best in Show, group placements, and sometimes Best of Breed or even points. Any cash prizes become the property of the handler, not the owner. Fees for showing at specialties are usually higher. Handlers make plans to attend shows based upon the number of clients booked for that show, so if you agree to have a handler take your dog, you are obligated to send it—or still pay the fee as though you did.

# Hired Hands

A successful handler can't do it alone. With a string of dogs, another set of hands is needed to groom and exercise dogs, have them ready ringside, and be ready to step in and show a dog should a conflict arise. These apprentice handlers work hard in exchange for a nominal salary and a foundation for their own future careers as professional handlers.

# Do-It-Yourselfers

The majority of people at the show receive no money for being there. They may have endured great hardship to travel to the show, slept in the back seat of their car, and sacrificed some other luxuries in order to afford the weekend. They are the owner handlers, the ones who are there because they love their dogs and they love the sport, not because someone is paying them to be there. Yet they are the most neglected and abused people at the show. The Owner Handler's

Association of America is a group of dedicated owner handlers who work to promote the interests of the do-it-yourselfer. As more people opt to show their own dogs, and to do it well, owner handlers cannot help but gain the recognition they deserve.

## Underdogs

Lowest on the food chain is the *novice*, a word far too often and unjustly uttered with such contempt that it rivals any four letter word in the English language. Yet, virtually every person at the show had to start as a novice! Everyone needs someone to look down on, and in the dog world the newcomer (as I prefer to call them) is the perfect target. One would think that other owner handlers would do everything they could to encourage newcomers, but for a variety of reasons the newcomer is often snubbed. The old-timers are either hard at work or too busy with their own agendas to even notice somebody new, and sometimes it's simply a case of bad timing. Old-timers can be just as nervous about showing as newcomers, and approaching them before

they go into the ring has been compared to approaching Olympic divers as they climb the high board and asking them where they bought their bathing suit; you probably wouldn't get a very helpful answer. Many newcomers are lost to the sport because of the rudeness of old-timers. If it happens to you, just remember: It has been my experience that the rudest ones are the ones with the least going for them.

*The owner handler typically shows only one or two dogs, but does it for the love of the breed and pride in a beloved pet. (Golden retriever)*

## Chapter Three

# Great Show Dogs Are Born...

The dog sitting beside you may be a beautiful animal and the apple of your eye. The chance of it just happening to be great show dog potential is slim, however, unless it was bred specifically for that purpose. You can try showing your best friend, as long as it is AKC-registered and has no disqualifying faults, and it may be a good idea to do so for fun and practice. But you probably will eventually want to find a more competitive dog and besides, your present dog will welcome a new buddy!

Note that your present dog can compete in a variety of other fields even if it is neutered or has disqualifying faults, as long as it is purebred and can receive an Indefinite Listing Privilege (ILP) number from the AKC. Non-AKC events may have more or less rigorous requirements for registration. Alternative competitions are described in the chapter entitled Other Worlds to Conquer (beginning on page 102).

## The Best of Breeds

The best breed to show is the breed you love, but if you have not yet decided just which breed you love the most, and want a breed that is also fun to show, consider some factors first:

*Many breeds require daily coat care, as well as hours of preparation before the show. Even the tousled-looking coat of the old English sheepdog is meticulously groomed.*

*Giant breeds entail special housing, feeding, and travel considerations, as well as a strong handler! (Great Pyrenees)*

### Hair of the Dog

Many of the most stunning breeds of dogs have coats that are especially eye-catching: the long, glamorous hair of the Afghan hound, the perfectly scissored coiffure of the poodle, or the crisp tailored coat of the wire fox terrier. Because hair is such an important part of these breeds, you must be willing to make sacrifices in order to keep such dogs in competitive coat. This may mean an extensive grooming commitment, with regular baths, brushing, and perhaps trimming or stripping. Don't expect to take a Maltese hiking one week and showing the next. Perfect long coats require everyday care. Those coats requiring trimming or stripping call for considerable talent and experience on the part of the groomer. You may be able to hire a handler to teach you to groom, but even so, don't expect your handiwork to be on a par with that of someone who has been grooming show dogs for a living for years. And don't expect to take your dog to the grooming parlor for a show clip; with few exceptions, groomers groom pets, not show dogs.

If your aim is to be competitive within a short time, avoid any breed that requires an exceptionally long coat, or a coat requiring cording, sculpting, or extensive trimming or stripping. Even some short coats need a surprising amount of grooming, so talk to breeders or handlers about grooming requirements.

### Size

Are you strong enough to control a Great Dane male when it spots a female in season? Are you agile

*Up, down, up, down: showing a small breed can be tough because of the repeated kneeling required. (Norwich terrier)*

enough to keep up with a German shepherd racing around the ring? Can you convince a Saint Bernard to put its feet where you want them? Showing a large dog requires that the handler be physically fit and sometimes quite strong.

Showing a small dog can be almost as challenging. Repeated kneeling and bending to pose a small dog can be extremely demanding and hard on the knees and back. Most small breeds must be lifted to a grooming table for the judge to examine.

Many physically challenged handlers have competed successfully in the ring by choosing breeds that can almost show themselves. Such breeds tend to be small to medium-sized, four-square breeds that bait easily but are not speedsters. The beagle, miniature pinscher, border terrier, Welsh corgi, and Shetland sheepdog are examples of breeds that might be shown from a wheelchair.

Small dogs are cute, and giant dogs are commanding, but think beyond your instinctive attraction to the practical aspects of dog mass. Small dogs are easier to transport, and their accessories and food cost less. These factors become important when you have many dogs, at which time you will wish you had chosen Chihuahuas.

## Popularity

If you already own a dog, chances are it is one of the more popular breeds, and chances are the show rings are swarming with these dogs. However, there are well over 100

breeds from which to choose, many of which are so unpopular that they may have no entries at all at most shows. The newcomer will find more success by avoiding both the most and the least popular breeds. Entries in the most popular breeds can be so large that the chances of even experienced handlers placing are slim; entries in the least popular breeds may be so limited that you never find any competition. You can get an idea of entries in your area by attending several local shows, perusing the AKC *Show Awards* publication, or by scrutinizing the point schedules (see page 92). The higher the point schedule, the more popular the breed.

## Professionalism

Some breeds are "handler breeds," that is, most of the dogs are shown by professional handlers, either because the competition is so

*Many sporting breeds are traditionally shown from a kneeling position. (Pointer)*

*Breeds that are traditionally shown "self-posed," such as the miniature pinscher, are popular choices for handlers restricted to wheelchairs.*

keen, the coat care so complex, or simply due to tradition. Doberman pinschers, poodles, cocker spaniels, and many terriers all have a large percentage of professionally handled entries. Your chances of winning at first with these breeds are much slimmer than with breeds that are principally owner handled, such as Chihuahuas, salukis, or American Eskimo dogs.

### Cropping

Some of the sharpest looking dogs have docked tails and cropped ears. Tails are docked shortly after birth, but ears may not be cropped when you bring home a puppy. You will have to locate a veterinarian with expertise in cropping your particular breed. A bad crop job can ruin a dog's chances for life. A show crop is not necessarily the same as a pet crop.

Cropping involves some pain and considerable post-surgical care, and

many people are morally opposed to it. In traditionally cropped breeds, uncropped dogs are not generally as successful in the ring as cropped dogs. Consider your feelings about cropping before buying a pup, and make sure you and your breeder agree about your plans to crop or not crop.

### Showmanship and Temperament

The standards of many breeds require that the tail and ears be held up, displaying the dog's happy and confident demeanor. Such confidence is not always easy to accomplish in a pet dog that only rarely goes to the hubbub of a dog show. The handler of the Irish wolfhound (in which the tail should be carried down) has one less worry than that of the bichon frise (in which the tail must be carried over the back). Breeds that are expected to bait, such as the collie or rottweiler, had better be trained to bait, whereas those in which baiting is not important, such as the basset hound or borzoi, again have one less worry.

Different breeds have different temperaments, although too often the show ring rewards the generic happy baiter, regardless of whether that temperament is typical or even desirable for that breed.

The most important temperament requirement for any breed is that the dog have a personality suitable for your family pet. Show time takes up only a small fraction of a dog's life— a few minutes of a couple of days every few weeks, over a period of a couple of years. For most show dogs the majority of their lives is still spent as a family pet. Pick a breed with a temperament you love to live with, and, pick a breed that you love. These are the most important breed requirements above all else.

Dog showing involves far too much work and sacrifice to go through it for anything less than your favorite breed. But you should go into it with your eyes open, and realize that, although it is possible to win with even the most difficult breed, some breeds are easier than others for newcomers.

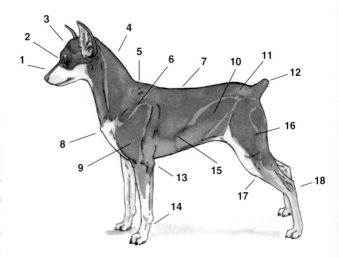

1. Foreface or muzzle, 2. Stop, 3. Skull, 4. Neckline, 5. Withers, 6. Shoulder, 7. Back, 8. Forechest, 9. Upper arm, 10. Loin, 11. Croup, 12. Tail, 13. Elbow, 14. Pastern, 15. Rib cage, 16. Thigh, 17. Knee, 18. Hock

*The external anatomy of the dog.*

# What Makes a Good Dog Good?

You can't find a good dog if you can't recognize a good dog. Recognizing a good dog comes with time and study. The most successful dog people never stop studying, and never stop learning. You can start now by learning the basics.

The basic guideline is the AKC standard for that breed, which describes the ideal specimen of a breed. It is the blueprint against which every dog is judged. The AKC has available a video version of the standard for every breed, which can help you visualize what the standard is describing. Most breeds have magazine or club newsletters that are full of photographs of dogs from many different kennels, some fitting the standard more than others.

Collect breed books and study the pictures and pedigrees.

# The Four Essentials

### Type

Adherence to the standard is called *type*: the general look of the dog, the headpiece, the silhouette, the coat, as well as the way of moving and the temperament. Contrast any two breeds, and you will find yourself speaking of type. For example, the typical (*typical* in this sense meaning correct for the breed) appearance, temperament, and movement for a German shepherd dog is different than for a Pekingese.

Those traits
that distinguish
a breed from
others are
referred to as
"type." This
dog's stocky
build, curly
coat, and
slightly
concave
topline help to
define it as a
Chesapeake
Bay retriever.

Besides the obvious differences in looks, the German shepherd dog moves in a flying trot, and is an alert, active dog, while the Pekingese is

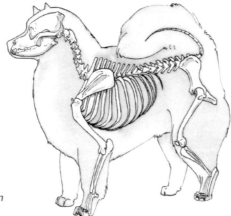

The skeleton of the dog.

required to move with a unique rolling motion and should have a haughty attitude.

As you get to know a breed, you will notice that even the most uniform breeds display considerable variation. Standards leave some room for interpretation, and different breeders favor different looks. These differences are usually described as different types within a breed, but as long as the dogs conform to the standard, they are all of the same type—the type of that breed. Such variations are more properly referred to as differences in *style*.

### Soundness

Unless the standard asks for something different, most breeds are expected to have an alert, friendly temperament, and move in a sound, efficient, ground-covering manner.

**From front or rear:** In most breeds, the legs are expected to reach to the ground in a straight line, when viewed either from the front or rear. When moving, the paws will tend to converge toward the center line with increasing speed, but the line they make from body to ground should still be straight. This is what the judge looks for when the dog moves "down and back." Viewed from the front, common problems are the elbows twisting outward, the pasterns flipping to the side, the toes pointing inward, or the entire assembly being loose or narrow. Viewed from the rear, common problems are moving cowhocked, or with the hocks close, bowlegged, or wide.

Practice watching dogs of all breeds trot. It takes considerably more work to discern soundness on long-coated dogs, but it can be done.

**Side movement:** Understanding correct side movement is a little more difficult. In most breeds the judge will look for a dog that trots easily and effortlessly, reaching far forward with the front legs and driving forcefully with the rear. To do so requires impeccable timing, balance, coordination, and condition. Common problems are lack of forward reach, high-stepping hackney movement, pounding the front feet into the ground, running as though going downhill, and lack of drive and extension in the rear. Variations on the theme are unlimited. Do not equate fast movement with good movement. If the legs are moving like pistons, especially if the other dogs in the ring are taking one step to every two, that dog does not have good side movement. An additional clue can be found by watching the topline of the dog; it should not bounce up and down when the dog moves. Bouncing indicates that energy is being expended to move the dog upward, rather than forward.

Take the time to understand movement; many people never do. These people tend to acquire dogs that don't move well, and they lose and their owners never understand why.

Many breeds have distinctive requirements for movement; for example, the miniature pinscher should have a hackney gait, the Ger-

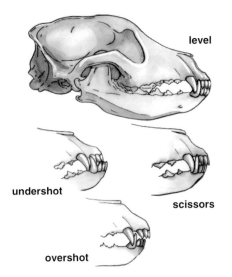

Four types of bite: level, scissors, undershot, and overshot.

man shepherd dog a flying trot, the Afghan hound a flowing "elastic" stride, and the chow chow a stilted gait with little reach and drive.

**Bone structure:** Correct bone structure is far more varied between breeds, but in most breeds it is desirable to have a neck that flows into the withers in a smooth line,

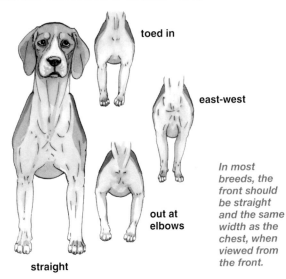

In most breeds, the front should be straight and the same width as the chest, when viewed from the front.

**19**

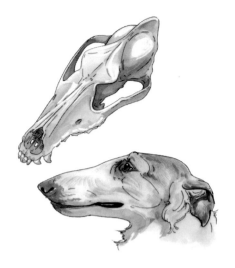

*Two extreme skull types: the dolicho-cephalic skull (borzoi) and the brachy-cephalic skull (bulldog).*

which then continues along a smooth, level topline to fall away somewhat in the croup. The chest is usually desired to be at least to the level of the elbow, and the angle formed by the scapula and upper arm is as close to 90 degrees as possible, with each situated at 45 degrees to the perpendicular. The rear is to be as equally angulated as the front. The feet should all point straight forward. There are many, many exceptions to the generic show dog just described, as outlined in each breed standard.

The neverending argument is that of type versus soundness. Type advocates contend that a mixed breed can move soundly, but it will always lack breed type. Soundness advocates point out that dog shows cannot be beauty contests, that a dog must be physically able to function and perform the job for which it was bred. Most people would agree

that a compromise is usually in order. No dog has it all. You will have to decide which is more important for you.

## Temperament

Two other integral aspects that are seldom described in breed standards are temperament and health; yet in real life both of these are far more important than a long stride or a long coat. Dogs were originally selected for their propensity to retrieve, chase, herd, guard, or perform other behaviors, and the temperament of dogs with proper breed type should indicate that they are able and eager to perform their breed's traditional task, even if that proper temperament sometimes proves to be at odds with your ideal of Lassie. Note that even Lassie's breed, the collie, has a propensity for unbridled barking—barking helps when herding. Other herders, such as corgis, may nip heels, sporting dogs may range tirelessly afield, sighthounds may chase anything that moves, and terriers may dig to China.

In most hunting breeds, dogs can prove their mettle at field trials. Field titles are awarded for pointing, retrieving, coursing, treeing, and trailing. Terriers can earn earthdog titles, and herding dogs can earn herding titles. All dogs can earn titles in obedience, tracking, and agility (see Other Fields to Conquer for a description of performance events and titles).

A dog of any breed should be able to perform the main duty of the modern dog: to be a trusted family pet. Make sure that your lifestyle is compatible with the temperament of your chosen breed, because it is not fair to either the individual dog or to the breed to expect it to abandon the temperament that enabled it to do its job for generations. This is another reason why it is preferable to visit the breeder's home and meet the prospective parents on their turf. If you don't like their temperaments, you should consider looking either for another breed or another breeder.

## Health

Good health is more difficult to evaluate. Many breeds are predisposed to certain health problems, either because particular physical characteristics predispose them to that problem, or because genes for a particular condition are more common within that breed's gene pool. Breeders should be able to tell you

*In most breeds, the rear should be straight and fairly wide as viewed from behind.*

**cow-hocked**

**bow-legged**

**straight**

how long other dogs in the pedigree lived and what health problems they had. They should also be willing to have you speak with their veterinarian.

In breeds with hip or shoulder problems, an Orthopedic Foundation for Animals (OFA) or PennHip evaluation should be available for breeding stock. Large, heavy breeds

*The way a dog moves is a product of both type and soundness. (German shepherd dog)*

*Correct bone structure should enable a dog to perform the task for which it was bred. (German shorthaired pointer)*

are more prone to hip and shoulder problems. Toy breeds are prone to knee problems (luxating patellas). In breeds with ocular problems, a recent Canine Eye Registration Foundation (CERF) number should be available. DNA testing is now available for a growing list of hereditary disorders, including progressive retinal atrophy in Irish setters, von Willebrand's disease in Scottish terriers, copper toxicosis in Bedlington terriers, and other disorders affect-

ing cocker spaniels, springer spaniels, and basenjis. It is vital that you be familiar with your chosen breed's health concerns.

Finding a dog with the four cornerstones of perfection—good type, soundness, temperament, and health—is not going to be an easy task. No dog is perfect. But that's what good breeders are striving for.

Talk to breeders, but do so with the ability to listen but not always believe. If everyone interpreted the standard and movement the same way, there would probably be no dog shows. Some breeders value certain traits more than others, some are stuck with certain traits and try to justify them, and some just plain don't have a clue and never will. Listen to their opinions, but in the end, trust yourself.

## A Good Dog Is Hard to Find

You will not find the show dog of your dreams in the local newspaper, a pet shop, a neighbor's litter, or by driving through the countryside and spotting a "puppies for sale" sign. Having stated this, there have been good, even great, show dogs obtained in each of these ways, but they were rare exceptions. Go with the odds and choose your dog from a reputable breeder with a solid background.

Contact the national breed club (their address is available from the

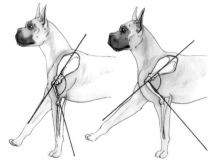

*The relationship between shoulder angulation and extent of front reach demonstrates that an upright shoulder blade restricts forward motion.*

AKC) and ask for a list of breeders. Ask also for information about breed books and magazines. Buy every one. Study every one.

If possible, attend a specialty show, preferably the National specialty for that breed. Here you will see the largest gathering of the year for that breed, and you can formulate your ideas of what style dog you like and what traits are most important to you.

Often, breeders will have puppies for sale at specialties, but fight the urge to bring one home. Impulse buying will undo all of the studying you have put into your effort. Don't pick a puppy simply because it is cute and available. Remember, you will want to see both parents so that you can evaluate their movement and temperament, and you should also be familiar with other dogs in the pedigree. It is better to find dogs that you really like and wait for them to have a litter than to fall for a puppy and hope it has a good background.

In most breeds there is considerable variation in style, and you should be true to yourself and choose the look you like best, even if it is not the most winning type. Just as with your choice of breeds, you will find the work much more worthwhile if you are promoting and showing a style you truly love and believe in. Keep in mind that dogs look different in photographs than they do in "person," so before making your final decisions make every effort to see the dogs from that line, and especially the parents, in the flesh.

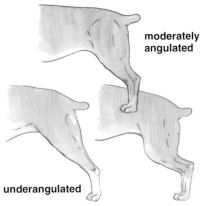

moderately angulated

underangulated

overangulated

*Although the preferred degree of angulation will vary between breeds, in most dogs a moderate degree is desirable, with either under- or over-angulated dogs faulty.*

## Credentials

It is difficult to make hard rules about choosing a breeder. The number of champions may indicate excellence in breeding, but it could also indicate overindulgence in breeding. In the best of worlds, a breeder would produce only a very few litters, and have most of the resulting puppies not only become champions, but top winners. A breeder who can produce quality from a few litters is a better bet than one who depends on sheer numbers for results.

As a newcomer, play it safe. Go to the established breeder with the proven record of champions and top winners. They may not necessarily have the best dogs, but the dogs will be good. They will probably have bred enough very good dogs that they can part with some of their best, and they may also be in a position to take a chance with placing a pup with a newcomer. At the same time, the disadvantage of buying from a large-scale breeding kennel is that

*Within every breed a wide variety of styles exist. (Akita)*

the breeder may simply not have enough time to spend coaching you. If they breed five litters a year, with five puppies in each, they would have 25 new owners to advise each year—on top of the ones from the previous five years or so! As much as they may want to chitchat on the phone about the cute antics of Junior, they may just not have the time. A small-scale, high-quality operation is usually the ideal, but can be more difficult to locate.

You can't expect breeders to give you the first choice from their top winning bitch, but at the same time, don't write your chances off of getting a puppy from such a bitch. Not all breeds have a waiting list of buyers, no matter how high quality the pups may be. Sometimes a breeder would rather place a pup in a loving home where it would be shown occasionally than in a large show kennel where it would not receive individual attention.

**Blue bloods and blue ribbons:** Much has been written on the merits (or lack thereof) of top winning dogs.

Campaigning a dog to top rankings can take tens of thousands of dollars, and is not in the budget of many serious breeders. Some of the best dogs are unadvertised, and even, unshown. Sometimes experienced fanciers of the breed will recognize the quality of these unsung dogs and use them for stud or acquire a puppy for themselves. Eventually you may come to do so, but now is not the time. There are too many breeders of poor quality dogs who use the lack of funds, or poor education of some judges, as their excuse for having nonchampion breeding stock. Play it safe and avoid dogs lacking credentials.

Do not be impressed by dogs listed in a prospective pup's pedigree that are further removed than its grandparents, and do not be overly impressed even by the grandparents. The most impressive generation of a pedigree should be the one closest to your new puppy.

### Proximity

In general, you are better off buying from local breeders than from remote ones. You will be able to see their dogs in the flesh, evaluate the dogs' movement and temperaments, and see the quality of dogs that they have sold to other exhibitors. You will be able to pick out your puppy yourself, rather than rely on photos or videos. Most important of all, the breeder will be available to coach you in grooming and showing, and in general act as your mentor. Other dogs from the same breeder are usually owned by local exhibitors, increasing the chance of making "dog friends" and of having other people interested in you and your dog.

What are the chances of finding the breeder and litter of your dreams in your area? Probably pretty small. Still, don't settle for less than the best just because the best isn't nearby. If you are convinced that the dogs are as good as they look in pictures, getting a dog from afar can be particularly exciting. If no other representatives from that kennel are in your area, the breeder will probably be particularly anxious to send a very good puppy to you. After all, that pup will act as ambassador for that kennel, and a good puppy will be worth tons of advertising for them.

Often, a dog from far away will not be of the same style as the local dogs, causing it to look out of place in the show ring. A good judge will not be fooled, however, and as long as it is sound and presented well you should not be held back. If the style you have chosen is more accepted by judges, you may just find yourself beating the locals on a regular basis, but the downside is that you may not be particularly popular with the local crowd as a result. Oh well, if you can't join 'em, beat 'em!

## Maturation Rate

If you are in a hurry to step into the show ring, you might consider maturity rates when choosing your dog. Some people argue that fast maturing dogs also become "over the hill" at a younger age. The only case where this is true is when the appearance of maturity is the result of carrying more weight while young. Dogs, like people, tend to put on weight as they age, and the dog that starts life fully fleshed out may be overweight when mature.

In general, smaller breeds, and smaller individuals within a breed, appear mature at a younger age than do larger dogs; meaty dogs tend to look more mature than do skinny dogs. Some lines within a breed will mature at a slower rate. The prime of life may not be until age four or five. But the standby excuse that "he's from a slow maturing line" is one of the most overused phrase at the dog show. In general, even if immature, a good dog will be basically good, and a bad dog will be basically bad. A bad dog will look less mature at any age because it will never move in a coordinated, sound fashion. Maturity will improve dogs, but it will not work miracles.

## Dog or Bitch?

If you have a preference, go for it. If not, consider these factors:

### The Dog

Males ("dogs") tend to be larger and more heavily coated than females ("bitches"), and of course, more masculine. Dogs will often be showier, entering the ring with a stallion-like attitude. Most dogs don't suffer from the moodiness that many bitches experience. In most breeds, the males do more winning than the bitches. In many breeds, however, they tend to be less well put-together than are the bitches.

## The Bitch

A bitch will have an estrus cycle every six months, during which time you will have to contend with her messy discharge and mate-alluring scent. Two months after each season, most bitches will experience a pseudopregnancy (false pregnancy), in which the nipples will swell and sometimes fill with milk, and her behavior may become somewhat melancholy or downright peculiar. In some cases, bitches will adopt toys as puppy surrogates. It can be difficult to show a bitch when she is in a false pregnancy, especially if it is a short-coated breed in which a sleek underline is important. No effective drug therapy is currently available. In coated breeds, bitches will usually lose ("blow") their coat after each estrus season.

Two drugs (marketed under the names Ovaban and Cheque drops) are available that can prevent estrus in bitches, but neither is without possible danger or side effects. They are not recommended for potential breeding stock because they can occasionally render a bitch infertile or more susceptible to pyometra, an infection of the uterus. Pyometra usually must be treated by immediate spaying of the bitch in order to save her life, although Herculean efforts may sometimes spare both her life and fertility in cases of "open" pyometra. If you have a bitch that you absolutely must breed, then you should not use these drugs.

## Breeding Considerations

Most people buy a bitch for their first show dog, perhaps with the idea of finishing her championship, breeding her, and starting their own line of famous dogs, or of making back their money. They seldom continue after breeding that one litter, because they find that their pups are not in demand and they are often stuck with a houseful of puppies and a fistful of bills. Disillusioned and overdogged, they drop out of the show world and wait for the puppies to die of old age so they can breathe again. Why? Because even though the bitch they bought was good enough to finish her championship, she was probably not really great or her breeders would have kept her for themselves. And the first-time breeders will not have had a chance to build a reputation with which to attract buyers. Unless they can depend on the bitch's breeders to refer buyers, it is unlikely that the puppy buyers will beat a path to their door.

## Quality

Starting with a dog instead of a bitch has several advantages. First, in most breeds it is easier to buy a good quality dog as more bitches than dogs are used for breeding. Only a small percentage of males will be selected to sire litters to a good many females. This means that breeders will tend to keep "better" bitches as potential breeding stock, but will only be tempted to keep the dogs. The result is that only fair bitches may be available for sale, but better dogs will be. In other words, it is usually easier for a newcomer to find a superior dog than it is a bitch.

But what about that dream litter? Having a dog will force you to postpone it, and that postponement will be the best thing that ever happened to you. If your dog is truly superior, another breeder may ask to use him at stud. If so, you have the pleasure of sharing in the resulting pups' wins without the worry of raising and placing them. You may also be able to get a stud fee puppy in order to continue with the next generation. During the process you will learn about breeding dogs and raising and placing puppies, and be exposed to many of the hidden pitfalls. When the time comes for you to take the plunge, you will be much wiser—perhaps wise enough to postpone it even further.

## Co-Ownerships

Sometimes breeders will sell bitches on a puppy-back agreement. Unless you know others who have worked with the breeder with no problems, and you know that you definitely want to breed a litter, this is seldom a good idea. You must consider the following:

- What if the bitch can't finish her championship?
- Where would the litter be born?

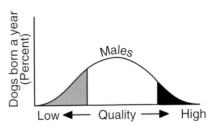

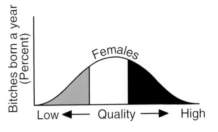

*The difference in quality between males and females commonly available for purchase by newcomers. The white area in each graph represents the available dogs.*

- Who would choose the stud and pay the stud fee?
- What would happen if there was only one puppy born?
- What if there is only one show-quality pup and the rest are pet quality?
- Who pays expenses?

Every possible scenario should be spelled out in writing before any agreement is made. If you can reach an understanding, however, a puppy-back arrangement may be a way to obtain a superior bitch, and it further assures you of the breeder's advice and help throughout.

Any co-ownership agreement should be in writing! Co-ownerships have caused too many disagreements because the exact terms of the agreement were never explicitly spelled out.

If you are making installment payments, the breeder will probably retain a co-ownership until the last installment, but sometimes a breeder will insist upon co-owning the puppy permanently. If the co-ownership is for insurance that the dog will be returned to the breeder in the event you cannot keep it, then such an agreement is usually acceptable.

In every breed there are intelligent and reputable breeders and an equal number of stupid and sleazy breeders. It is sometimes difficult to tell them apart. When you get your puppy you will be acquiring your pup's breeders as sort of "in-laws." Be careful!

# That Doggy in the Window

Now that you have selected the breeder, and possibly, the litter of your choice, how do you choose your future wonder pup? Start by telling the breeder what traits and characters are most important to you, and which of them is an absolute must. This should narrow your choices somewhat. Some pups may already be reserved. Ask to see them, and ask the breeder to point out why they were already chosen. Even the best litters seldom have every pup turn out to be top show potential. If the pups left to choose from are of so much poorer quality than the ones already chosen, you may be better off to postpone getting a puppy, and ask to be put higher on the reservation list for the

breeder's next litter. More often you will be confronted by a gaggle of wriggling cuties that all look pretty much the same to you. You can try to evaluate fronts, rears, angulation, movement, and bone size, but it can be difficult with these wiggleworms. Puppy aptitude tests have become popular for testing potential temperament; however, studies have shown that these tests have limited predictive value. Your best bet is to rely on the breeder, who has studied the puppies' conformation and personalities every day since birth, and is familiar with how that line matures.

Another option is to hire an experienced dog person, usually a professional handler who is familiar with your breed, to evaluate the puppies and choose one for you. Most breeders will allow you to return a puppy if you are not satisfied with it, although you will be liable for any shipping fees and other expenses. Some warnings, though. You can become attached to a puppy overnight. Especially if you have children, don't count on sending a pup back, no matter how disappointed you are with its quality. And, how will you evaluate the puppy? All of your studies have probably centered around the qualities you should look for in adults. Different lines within a breed mature differently, so that it can be difficult to come up with guidelines that will fit all puppies of a breed. Asking local breeders to evaluate a puppy from afar may not be the best idea, especially if the local breeders have their own litters to place, or may see you as future competition. Again, you can ask a professional handler for an opinion, but he or she may not be an expert in your breed. In general, you must rely on your own opinion, and if you have done your homework up to that point, and have not received the pup totally sight unseen, it's usually best to stick to your initial impressions about the litter and keep your pup. It's easy to feel uneasy about your choice, but remember that the most important quality your pup can have is that of being a good pet. If you fall in love with it, then it is perfect.

When I chose my first saluki, I studied and agonized and finally picked a dog from a large kennel on the other side of the country. When we opened the door of the shipping crate, out stepped a short-legged dog that looked more like a beagle than a saluki. It suddenly dawned on me that I didn't have the slightest idea of how a saluki puppy should look, so I took him to the local breeders for an opinion. They all had an opinion of him—bad, send him back. But no two breeders agreed on what made him bad. We went to a match where he placed fifth out of five. The other puppies there were perfect miniature salukis; mine still looked like a beagle. Meanwhile, I did what I had vowed I would not let happen: I fell in love with my "awful" puppy. I decided to keep him as an obedience dog, and my dreams of a show dog went up in smoke. Until, that is, he finished his championship at the age of ten months (beating all the local dogs), and later became a top 10 show dog! He didn't look like a beagle anymore.

## Adult Dogs

The best way to predict how a puppy will mature is to *wait* until it is mature. If you absolutely must have a winning dog, buy an adult, or even a finished champion. One warning though: Many dogs are only good enough to finish their championships, but will never win at the Best of Breed (BOB) level of competition. If you want a dog to show, buying such a dog is a very poor choice because it will not be competitive. If you plan to buy a dog that can compete at the BOB level, have a professional handler find such a dog for you. However, most people would rather take the chance and have the fun of raising their future champion from puppyhood.

## The Interview

When you speak to the breeder, be prepared to tell him or her exactly what you want in a dog. Also be prepared to answer a number of questions about your facilities and intentions. In fact, a sign of a responsible breeder is one who wants to know how the dog will live, what has happened to any of your previous dogs, and why you want a dog of that breed in the first place. Don't try to mislead the breeder about your experience; a good breeder is anxious to work with a sincere newcomer. On the other hand, don't expect breeders to part with their best puppy to a novice; most have learned that many newcomers promise the world but often soon lose interest in showing or in the dog itself. A good breeder should value a loving home over an illustrious show career, but will want both.

The key to communicating with breeders is honesty, both to yourself and the breeder. Don't make promises you can't keep. Ask yourself how many shows you can reasonably expect to attend, and what you will do if the dog does not meet your expectations. Can you keep the dog in proper condition, especially if a lot of exercise or coat care is required? If the breeder wanted to take the dog and show it on occasion, would you be willing to send your dog away from home? Could you afford to hire a handler if needed?

How *not* to impress a breeder:

- By pretending you know everything about the breed. The breeder will expect you to know something about the breed, but you are not expected to cram years of knowledge into a few months of study. If you aren't familiar with a particular dog or concept, admit it.
- By pretending you have experience that you don't really have with showing dogs. Breeders have a worldwide network of other breeders. If you try to claim you showed Tanzanian coonhounds in Budapest, chances are by the end of the week the breeder would have found out that not a single Tanzanian coonhound breeder in Budapest ever heard of you.
- By throwing off on other breeders. If you don't like a certain look or line, that's fine to say, but don't "trash" dogs or breeders.
- By starting a conversation with "How much?" This is not to say that this is not a reasonable question, but don't make it sound as though price is your number one priority. No breeder wants to think you chose their pup because it was the bargain basement special. At the same time, for most people money is a consideration, and most breeders will work with you if yours seems like an ideal home.
- By being in a hurry. Good breeders don't typically breed unless they have a number of reservations for puppies. You shouldn't expect them to have a good puppy available at your call. To get the best pup, and to make the best impression, get on the list to reserve a pup from an upcoming litter. And wait—impatiently!
- By telling the breeder you just want a winner. A good breeder will worry about the pup's future if it doesn't turn out to be a world beater. Even the best bred and most promising puppy may not always mature as expected.
- By making promises you can't possibly keep. Most breeders have heard it all before. Make realistic promises that you really do intend to live up to.

Purchasing a puppy under false pretenses and expectations will eventually cause many hard feelings. Don't ask for a top show-quality puppy, make promises to show it, and then never get around to it or give up after a couple of red ribbons in the puppy class. Give the dog and the breeder a chance. Most breeders lose money on every puppy in every litter they breed. They breed as a labor of love, with one of the few rewards being the puppy's success in the show ring. Often, years of study and work have gone into the creation of your puppy, and that pup may carry irreplaceable and valuable genes.

If you don't intend to show your dog, don't get a show-quality dog. You can still get a gorgeous representative of the breed that is nonetheless not show quality.

At the same time, don't get a pet-quality pup with the intention of showing it. Again, one of the reasons for breeding is to enhance the reputation of the breeder's line by having the best stock appear in the show ring. Showing a pup the breeder deemed less than the best can place the breeder in an embarrassing predicament, as other breeders will assume the pup was sold to you as show quality. If you do have a pup that was sold as pet quality, and then decide you would like to try showing, contact the breeders and ask their opinion. They may take a look at your pup and decide it turned out better than expected, or they may offer to get you started with a show-quality companion for your first dog.

## The Breeder's Questions

Don't be offended if the breeder asks for references or names of other breeders who have sold you dogs in the past. They will also want a description of your facilities, and may insist upon inspecting it personally, and they may want to meet your family, especially if you have children. All of these invasions into your privacy are signs of a good breeder. The breeder may be uncomfortable giving you the third degree, but has learned the hard way that the ones who pay the price for politeness are the pups who end up in a home that was not suitable.

Incidentally, one assumed requirement that most breeders have is that you stay in touch with them throughout the life of your new dog. Part of the breeder's reward is hearing about how the pup just learned to swim, or won its first point, or hogs the whole bed at night. And sad though it may be, the breeder hopes to receive a tearful call 10 or 15 years in the future that your beloved family pet finally succumbed to old age.

## Chapter Four

# Great Show Dogs Are Made...

The best of genes can make the best of dogs only if accompanied by the best of care and training. Good care entails proper veterinary attention, nutrition, exercise, and grooming. Good training entails proper socialization and show practice.

## Veterinary Care

Show dogs come in contact (either directly or by way of the judge's hands) with thousands of other dogs from various parts of the country, and as such are exposed to many more communicable diseases than the average dog. As essential as proper vaccinations are to every dog, they are vital to the show dog.

**Weight and coat:** The show dog's weight and coat must be perfect; internal and external parasites can play havoc with both. Scratching can cause extensive hair loss and matting. Again, as crucial as parasite control is with any dog, it is critical with the show dog.

**Flaws and scars:** Small flaws and scars that would be insignifi-

cant to the pet dog can seriously detract from the show dog's image. It is a certainty that any major laceration will occur on the "show side" (side facing the judge), so you may need to have even small wounds sutured. Unless told otherwise, veterinarians are notorious for clipping away gobs of coat in order to suture the smallest of cuts, so make it clear that your dog's coat must be preserved if at all possible.

**Lameness:** Subtle lameness will not go unnoticed in the show ring and may need the attention of an orthopedic specialist. It can be difficult and frustrating to try to return a lame dog to 100 percent soundness, and veterinarians know that most pet owners are unwilling to invest the time, money, and effort in alleviating a slight hitch in the gait. Your veterinarian needs to know that your situation is different and must be familiar with your dog's requirements as a show dog, and aware that you cannot settle for "good enough" when that could mean the end of your dog's show career.

**Docking and cropping:** In breeds in which docking and cropping are required, it is absolutely essential that the veterinarian in charge be experienced with that breed. If need be, travel to a veterinarian who has a reputation for proper cropping. A talented and experienced veterinarian can enhance a dog's appearance by tailoring a crop to an individual dog's conformation.

Many veterinarians are themselves involved in showing dogs, and thus understand the particular requirements of your dog. Others have gained a reputation for their ability and understanding of the needs of the show dog, and are the choice of most serious exhibitors in the area. Ask these exhibitors which veterinarian they prefer, and then make an appointment to get acquainted. If you have a breed with specific health concerns, try to find a veterinarian who is familiar with those concerns and has other dogs of that same breed as patients.

# Nutrition

Dogs can survive on any food that meets the minimum requirements set forth by the American Association of Feed Control Officers (AAFCO). Your show dog needs to do more than survive, however; it needs to blossom.

At your first visit to a dog show you will no doubt visit the dog food booths, pick up a free sample of food, and talk to the representative who will make you feel like the worst dog owner on earth for feeding your dog tripe from the grocery store. The foods marketed at the show usually contain premium ingredients, boast premium nutritional analyses, and can be yours for a premium price. They will not miraculously transform your ugly duckling into a swan, however. Many top winning dogs eat high-quality (but not premium) dog foods from reputable companies.

Dog owners tend to be one of three types when it comes to feeding their dogs: the first tries to save a buck by feeding dog food made from sawdust and corncobs, and then wonders why the dog has to eat so much of it and has a coat like straw; the other extreme chooses a food because it costs the most and is made from bee pollen, llama milk, and caviar yolks (and of course, no preservatives), and then wonders why the food is rancid half the time and their dog is a blimp; and the third type buys a high-quality food from a recognized source and has healthy dogs to show for it.

## Feeding Trials

In choosing any food, the first rule is to select a food that states on the label not only that it meets the requirements set by the AAFCO, but also has been tested in *feeding trials*. Some of the smaller dog food companies have a blend of ingredients that look like they should be good, but have never actually been tested on dogs. Don't let your dog be the guinea pig—feed a high-quality food from a name-brand company.

### Protein

Many high-quality foods boast of being high in protein, and with good reason. Protein provides the necessary building blocks for growth and maintenance of bones, muscle, and coat, and in the production of infection-fighting antibodies. Meat-derived protein is more highly digestible than plant-derived protein, and is of higher quality. The quality of protein is as important as the quantity of protein.

Puppies and adolescents need particularly high protein levels in their diets, which is one reason they are best fed a food formulated for their life stage. Older dogs, especially those with kidney problems, should be fed lower levels of very high-quality protein. Studies have shown that high-protein diets do not cause kidney failure in older dogs, but given a dog in which kidney stress or decompensation exists, a high-protein diet will do a lot of harm. If your show dog is active throughout the day, or is underweight, you may want to feed it a high-quality protein food.

### Fat

Fat is the calorie-rich component of foods, and most dogs prefer the taste of foods with higher fat content. Fat is necessary to good health, aiding in the transport of important vitamins and providing energy. Dogs deficient in fat often have sparse, dry coats. A higher fat content is usually found in puppy foods, while overweight dogs should be fed a lower fat food. Many high-protein foods also have a high fat content.

Ask professional handlers what they feed their dogs. If you like the condition of their dogs, try that same food with yours. Always consider whether your dog is underweight or overweight for its breed, and adjust both the type and amount of food accordingly.

# Exercise

Proper nutrition is required to supply the building blocks for muscle and coat, but proper exercise and coat care are required to get your dog into proper condition. Judges take into consideration the conditioning of the dogs put before them, and constantly lament the lack of muscle

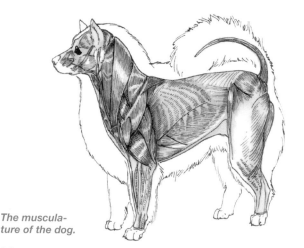

*The musculature of the dog.*

tone so common in many breeds. Far too many show dogs spend their lives in cages and kennel runs. Coated breeds are often not allowed to run on grass for fear of damaging hair, and short-haired breeds are not allowed to run with playmates for fear of receiving bites and scratches. Our observations have shown that dogs raised with limited exercise grow into terribly unsound adults, and that dogs raised with unlimited, but not forced, exercise grow into sound (or fairly sound!) adults.

On the other extreme is the exhibitor, far less common, who goes overboard with the idea that exercise will transform their dogs into paragons of soundness. They roadwork the dog until it is muscle-bound and, usually, far less sound than it would have been. Like the jogger who seems to always have an injury, the over-conditioned dog can develop a myriad assortment of joint problems.

Finding the right amount of exercise can be a challenge. Never roadwork a puppy, or require any dog to exercise past the point at which it wants to stop. Swimming is an excellent exercise for the overweight dog, but never push it past the point of exhaustion, which could be dangerous.

Doggy treadmills are available so that dogs can trot in all weather without mussing their hair; some handlers even carry them along in their rigs so that the dogs in their care can exercise while on the dog show circuit.

## Grooming

Every breed of dog requires far more grooming than you would think, and each breed has such specific needs that it would be impossible to list them here. In general, however, the number one requirement is that the dog be clean. Even in breeds in which the standard states that they should be shown in a natural state, that natural state should be a dirt-, odor-, and parasite-free one.

Have your breeder show you how to groom your dog, or hire a handler to show you the general procedure. Other exhibitors within your breed can also show you the ropes, but don't expect them to divulge any closely guarded secrets. You'll have better luck by getting to know people in another breed that has a similar coat to your dog's breed. Visit the dog show

*Almost every breed requires considerably more grooming than meets the eye. (West Highland white terrier)*

vendors and ask their advice about what products would be ideal for your dog. Most vendors know their products well and won't sell you too much more than you need.

### Using Foreign Substances

The AKC regulations state that dogs cannot have any foreign substances in their coat when they compete, and that any cleaning substances must be removed from the coat before entering the show ring. The limits of this rule are constantly being pushed by exhibitors, however. White legs are customarily chalked or powdered before competition in order to appear whiter. The excess powder is brushed away, and most judges overlook the remaining slight residue—but some do not and will not hesitate to order such a dog from the ring. Cornstarch can also add body to long hair, but again, if the dog shakes and is enveloped by a dust storm, expect to be asked to leave.

*A beautiful coat is the result of good nutrition, good care, and good genes! Show dogs—especially long coated white ones—require special attention to eye, ear, and oral hygiene. (Maltese)*

Most exhibitors and judges accept a little white powder, but the use of dyes to change or "enhance" coloring is not acceptable under anyone's rules. Some exhibitors do secretly apply a kaleidoscope of false colors, however. Avoid joining their ranks. Equally illegal, but widespread, is the use of nose blackening agents.

Hair spray is technically not allowed, but for some breeds (such as poodles), the use of some spray is acceptable. Use as little as possible and use a brand that leaves no sticky residue. Spray left in the coat can cause coat breakage, so sprayed dogs should be washed after being shown.

## Coat Types

**Short haired breeds** usually require some trimming to tidy up scraggly hairs under the tail and belly and under the neck. Those with thick, short coats may need to be stripped in order to pull out some of the undercoat. A shedding blade can help to smooth such coats during shedding season.

**Wire coats** usually require hand plucking and stripping. Clipping a wire coat exposes the soft undercoat, ruining the desired harsh texture. The harsh texture can also be lost by washing the dog before showing it. Special shampoos are available that will not soften the coat as much. Preparation of the terrier coat is an artistic talent that

you cannot expect to develop without help.

**Long coats** usually require washing and being blown dry. The best hair dryers force cool air to dry the dog, but these are expensive and you can start with your own hand-held blow dryer (using the cool or warm setting). If you have a dog that requires extensive drying, you may wish to eventually invest in a high-quality dryer. Gently brush the coat as the dryer blows upon it. This process will straighten the coat and cause it to have more body. Long coats must be kept clean. Dirt and oil will cause the coat to tangle and mat, and mats cause hair loss. Washing a long coat two or three times a week is considered normal.

Long-coated breeds may need to have their coats wrapped. Each breed has a different technique, but one common method is to brush the coat straight, wrap it with a sheet of wax paper, then fold that wrapped tress back on itself and secure it with a tiny rubber band. Ear fringe is sometimes wrapped with Vet-Wrap (a veterinary bandage that clings to itself), or it may be protected by a "snood" (an elasticized fabric tube that fits around the neck, holding the ears away from the face). In males, the coat on the sides may be held out of the way of any urine by securing the coat to the side with a hair styling clip. Dog show exhibitors have proven themselves to be remarkably resourceful when it comes to

*Also dressed for success, this Afghan sports a "snood" around its ears and hair clips around its belly hair. The snood prevents the long hair of the ears from dragging in food and water, or from being accidentally chewed off by the dog. The clips hold the coat out of harm's way when the male dog lifts its leg.*

ways of protecting hair, so keep your eyes and ears open for ideas, and ask.

*"Who's the fairest of them all?" It would be impossible to achieve the bouffant hair-do of the poodle without considerable grooming talent—and a slight misting of hairspray. (Standard poodle)*

# Details

**The vibrissae (whiskers)** of most breeds are traditionally cut off for the show ring so that the head has a cleaner look to it. Some exhibitors feel strongly that the vibrissae are important sensory organs functioning to protect the eyes from sticks and branches, and perhaps even affecting balance. Although still in the minority, these exhibitors refuse to cut the vibrissae and judges should never penalize them for that decision. In some breeds, such as the American Eskimo dog and saluki, the vibrissae are traditionally never cut.

As you become more familiar with your breed standard, and with the areas in which your dog may not quite measure up to it, you may be able to groom your dog to compensate for those shortcomings. Always experiment a long time before a show, giving the hair time to grow back, or try slicking the hair down to get an idea of how it would look shorter. If possible, trim the right (non-show) side of the dog only and leave it for a day or two. Study the effect it creates before trimming the left (show) side.

*Most breeds need a little trimming in order to give a neater look, especially around the feet. The backs of this borzoi's hocks have been scissored and then combed down, and the scraggly hairs around the toes have been cut away.*

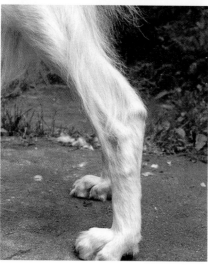

I once decided that a borzoi I was showing needed a longer neck, so I trimmed and thinned and brushed and finally believed I achieved a longer looking neck. When we won Reserve, the judge commented that she would have gone Winners except that her neck was far too long! Watch out—you may get what you ask for!

**The teeth** of any dog should be kept clean for the sake of its health. A show dog's teeth must also be clean for the sake of appearance; a dog with tartar teeth is a dog that has no place in the show ring.

**Ears and eyes** must also be cared for, both for health and appearance's sake. A dog with ear problems can scratch its hair out, shake its head, hold its head sideways, or just plain be in too much pain to show. Eye discharge can signal a number of ocular anomalies or problems, and should not be ignored. Tears react with oxygen to form a red stain on the fur. Tear stain removers are available but must be used diligently. The same principle applies to saliva stains around the mouth. In fact, red stain anywhere on the dog can be a sign of excessive licking in that area, and may be cause for veterinary attention.

**Toenails** of the show dog are cut at least once a week, and are kept shorter than those of most household pets. Dogs that object to nail clippers may be more tolerant of a nail grinder (a Dremel hand-grinding tool with a sanding drum, available at your hardware store). Take care that any long hair does not become wrapped around the shaft; you can put the dog's foot in a nylon stocking and poke the nails through if your dog has long hair on its feet.

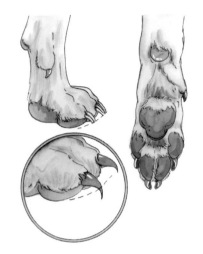
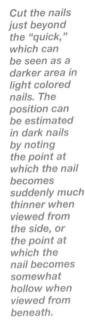

*Cut the nails just beyond the "quick," which can be seen as a darker area in light colored nails. The position can be estimated in dark nails by noting the point at which the nail becomes suddenly much thinner when viewed from the side, or the point at which the nail becomes somewhat hollow when viewed from beneath.*

plete stranger, the show dog must be neither overwhelmed, shy, out of control, nor aggressive.

Socialization begins in the whelping box, with gentle handling by the breeder. Between the ages of 8 and 12 weeks, puppies should be exposed to as many situations as possible. Early experiences should be pleasant and short. Many obedience clubs offer puppy kindergarten classes that can be beneficial for the single dog that

## Socialization

The show dog is expected to perform in ways that the average pet is never asked to do. Hustled through a crowd of strange dogs and people, thrust into a line of other dogs, and groped by a com-

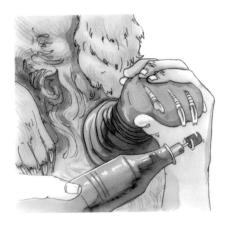

*When using a nail grinder on a dog with long hair, place the foot in a stocking and push the nails through it. The stocking will prevent the fair from becoming tangled in the grinder.*

has no housemates to play with. Anything you can do at an early age to build self-confidence and happiness in a variety of situations will be the foundation for a real show dog.

# Training

## Classes

Most kennel clubs offer handling classes, providing a wonderful opportunity for your dog to become comfortable around other people and dogs. In a good class you may even learn how to handle. Don't expect the person teaching the class to be an expert on your breed, but most of the time the instructor will know more about showing any breed of dog than you will. Don't use training class to train your dog. Work on the basics at home, so your dog already knows what is expected of it before it gets to class. Class should be used for socialization and as a dress rehearsal, not as a place to further confuse your dog.

Most handling classes, however, are too crowded to be of much help to the handler half of the team, and they can actually hurt the dog half. Too often, dogs are expected to remain posed for minute after minute while awaiting their 30 seconds in the spotlight. Such experiences can snuff the enthusiasm right out of a dog.

Don't make your dog remain posed in a large class. Practice baiting while waiting. Many nervous dogs will spit the bait right out in class (and at shows), so if you can get your dog eating and then baiting in class, you have achieved a valuable goal, both in terms of having a dog that is obviously more at ease, and a dog that will bait for you in the ring. Some other dogs will be too excited to be around potential new friends to bait, so they need the repeated exposure in order to calm down and pay attention to you.

Most classes last for an hour, which is far too long for any dog to be expected to stay on its toes. If your dog gets tired, take it back to the car and let it go to sleep, or go home. Don't give your dog a chance to experience being tired and dull while on the show lead.

Don't forget to train your dog to ride quietly in a cage to and from class. A show dog must learn to relax in a cage, for its own safety and your peace of mind.

## Training Tips

Judges sometimes say they could not deny a dog a win because it "asked for it." Dogs ask for wins by strutting and showing, that is, by having a good attitude. Most dogs handled by newcomers have a bad attitude because their owners have emphasized compliance over fun.

I was competing with my new champion puppy for the first time, mortified that he kept grabbing the lead and trying to play tug-of-war. A well-known handler next to me commented on my dog's wonderful attitude and how she wished her dog was like that. I thought she must be quite insane. With time I trained my dog to behave and then spent much of the rest of his show career dragging him around the ring. Once in a while his old mischievous self would resurface and he was unbeatable. If only I had paid attention to what that handler was really telling me...

Leash training begins at birth with gentle handling and proper socialization. It continues the first time you put your puppy on leash. When your pup first feels that strange string around its neck, it won't be so sure it likes this new game. Use a wide non-choke adjustable show lead-type combination leash/collar, or any wide soft collar and lightweight lead. Train before a meal, and stock your pockets with treats. Those soft/moist cat and dog treats are very handy, or you can even use the regular dog food that comes in soft/moist chunks. Walking on lead should be a real treat for your pup.

Don't ever drag your pup around by the leash. Not only is it bad show training, but it's cruel. Instead, entice it with a treat. A few steps forward earns it a tidbit. Increase the number of required steps a few at a time. When the brakes are applied, try another direction. If you have more than one puppy or dog, let them watch each other being trained. They will be clamoring for their turn!

Remember to make gaiting fun. Reward your pup for trotting proudly with its head held high. When it breaks into a gallop, slow down but don't give either a correction or a reward. Quit well before your dog is ready for the game to be over.

**Posing:** Now for the hard part: posing. Everybody has seen pictures of little four-week-old puppies posing like Best in Show dogs. That always seems kind of dumb. Puppies should not be expected to pose like a pro. Again, the emphasis should be on attitude.

With your trusty treats, walk your dog to a gradual stop. Place your

*"Show me!" (Saluki)*

*You can train a pup to pose by standing it so that it spans a gap between two chairs. Place a pillow below in case of an accidental slip, but don't let an accident occur!*

left hand in front of its hind leg, and your right hand in front of its nose, holding a treat. After your pup stands still (sort of) for a few seconds, reward it. Most puppies will naturally stop with their rear legs well under themselves. That's OK

*You can train a small dog to pose by standing it over a cold can and steadying its rear.*

for now. Puppy legs aren't strong enough to support them properly when stretched out behind. Just work on trying to keep your dog focused on the treat and sort of standing for now.

The number one mistake made by most new handlers is to emphasize obedience at the expense of attitude. Most people teach the dog to stand still by repeatedly correcting it when it moves its feet. An easier and gentler way is to have the dog teach itself. You can do this by posing the dog over a log or can (the dog will be less inclined to rest its belly on the can if the can is chilled), or even between two chairs with a small gap between them. If you choose the latter method, take care to *never*, under any circumstances, let your pup fall. Pose your dog with its front legs on one side of the barrier or gap, and rear legs on the other. If it tries to step forward with its rear legs, it will either be met by an object or by thin air (again, let it feel that the floor is gone, but don't let it fall). Now entice the dog forward with the bait. Gradually train it to stretch out by requiring it to step forward a little more each time in order to reach the treat.

Now position the legs by hand, all the while letting the pup nibble the bait in your right hand. When the pup moves a leg from position, simply remove the bait. As long as the legs are left where placed, continue to reward. Only when your pup knows the routine should you

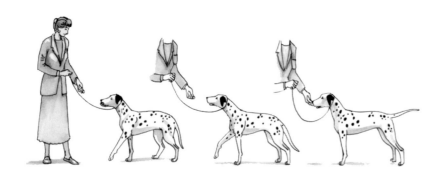

remove the treat and require the pup to look at it for a couple of seconds before giving a reward. Work up to longer time periods. If your dog is posting, lure it slightly forward with the bait before rewarding it.

Your dog should now really be looking forward to its show training sessions. Free food! Or at least the most easily earned food ever. All that is required is to trot and stand and look happy. What an easy job!

**Baiting:** One way to keep your dog attentive in the ring is to teach it how to catch bait. This is not a trick for a young pup, but most chow hounds can learn to catch fairly easily. Stand a few feet in front of your dog. Toss a bit of bait in an arc calculated to land between the dog's nose and eyes. Chances are the bait will bounce right off and the dog will simply look stupid. Grab the bait off the ground before your dog can reach it. Repeat. Eventually you will come to the conclusion that yours is the dumbest dog ever born, as piece after piece hits it in the head, but at some point a neuron will fire, and

your dog will have an idea: "If I grab the food in midair my owner won't have a chance to grab it off the ground." Once the idea clicks, you just have to practice a few more times and you will have a dog that is always on its toes when it thinks it's trick time.

Some breeds are traditionally baited into a stance, rather than being hand-posed. The collie breeds are the best example of this technique. Stand in front of your dog. Practice "leading it by the nose" by moving the bait right or left. Notice that when you move the bait to the dog's right, the left leg moves forward and toward the center line. You can position the dog's front legs by maneuvering the bait right and left. Eventually, require your dog to pose itself before rewarding it, and to stand for longer periods before getting the reward. Baiting can keep your dog alert during a long class, and helps your dog to show itself.

**The examination:** After your dog is happily posing, you can start to accustom it to the procedure of

*Using a treat, such as cooked liver, to attract the dog's attention is helpful in keeping the dog alert and happy while in the ring. (Samoyed)*

testicles in males. Some dogs will take it all in stride, but most need a little practice to either learn to stop wiggling, licking, and jumping up on this nice person who seems to want to pet them all over, or to learn not to shrink and duck away from this stranger with a suspicious interest in their body. For the overly excitable type, practice makes perfect. The "judge" should go over the dog quickly and without any sweet talk. If the dog can hold still, the handler should then praise and reward it with a tidbit. The shy dog should follow the basic procedures outlined for shyness on pages 97–100; the "judge" should give a cursory examination, once again without sweet talk, but should give the dog a tidbit after the exam. Initial examinations for all dogs should be short and sweet: a lifted lip, pat on the head, a stroke on the back, and that's it. Work up to a more realistic exam only when the cursory exam is mastered.

being touched by a stranger. The judge will lift the dog's lips to look at its teeth, and in some breeds will even open the mouth. Then the judge will work gradually toward the rear of the dog, feeling the body and legs, perhaps picking up a foot, and checking for the presence of two

# Chapter Five
# What Every Good Handler Must Know

## Basic Handling

**B**efore stepping one foot into a show ring you will want to make sure you know where to put both your feet and your dog's feet. In other words, do your homework. Your neighbors will have to get used to seeing you run back and forth in the street time after time. Any sport requires some lonely hours of practice, and showing a dog is no exception.

You need a lot of practice to be good; your dog will probably not need nearly as much. If you have another dog, even a mutt, use it to practice with so you don't bore your future star to death. Besides, the more experience you have with different dogs, the more you will come to know your own.

Showing a dog consists of two major challenges: posing (or "stacking") the dog, and moving (or "gaiting") the dog.

### Posing

One of the most commonly uttered phrases at dog shows is "You should see this dog in the backyard. You can't really see it here, but he's just stunning at home." Your aim in posing your dog is to attain that same stunning look you see in your own backyard.

With only a few exceptions (most notably German shepherd dogs), the standard pose is with the front legs perpendicular to the ground and parallel to each other. Feet should point straight forward (in most breeds). The toes of the rear feet should also point straight ahead. The hocks of the rear legs

*The goal: To have our dogs look as good in the show ring as they do at home or in the field. (Saluki)*

should be perpendicular to the ground and the entire leg should be parallel to its mate.

How wide? In general, the front legs should be placed so that they are the same width as the chest. Set the legs so that the elbows are snug to the sides of the body; if set too wide, there will be a gap between the elbow and body. Rear legs, too, should be set so that they go toward the ground in a straight line. Again, the legs should be parallel to one another.

Don't just grab the feet and try to plop them into position. It won't work. Instead, with your dog on lead, walk it slowly into a sort of pose. Then perform the following steps:

1. Place your right hand under the dog's chin.
2. With your right hand, pull the dog toward you very slightly, shifting its weight off its left side.
3. Place your left hand immediately below the dog's left

elbow, and move the dog's leg into position.
4. Before letting go of the left leg, use your right hand to push the dog's weight back onto its left side.
5. Push the dog's weight off its right side.
6. Place the right front leg into position, guiding it from just below the elbow.
7. Shift the dog's weight back to midline and release the leg.
8. With your right hand still under the dog's chin, run your hand along the dog's side or back until you get to its rear left leg. You can eventually omit this step as the dog comes to expect the next step.
9. Grasp the leg around the "knee" (stifle) and move it into position. In a large dog, you will have to push the weight off that leg first.
10. Reach under the dog's belly, grasp the left stifle, and position the left rear leg.

*3. After setting the front, grasp the left rear leg by the stifle (knee) or hock (in a small dog), and place it into position, with the paw facing forward and the hock perpendicular to the ground.*

*4. Finally set the right rear leg parallel to the left rear leg.*

**11.** Recheck the front.

**12.** Now hold the head up high, and *voila*! A show dog handler is born!

Practice posing your dog until you can get it into position in about ten seconds. Always set the legs in the same order: left front, right front, left rear, right rear. The left legs are posed first because they are on the judge's side. Keep your dog happy while practicing with liberal use of treats, praise, and play. Keep in mind that the closer you can get your dog to posing itself the less you have to do.

**Exceptions:** For giant breeds, you may not be able to keep a hand on the chin when you go to set the rear. Just try to steady the dog by touching its side or chest.

For small breeds, posing for the judge is usually done both on the floor and on the table. It will be easier to set the rear by reaching over the back or from behind rather than under the dog. You must accustom your small dog to posing on the table

without any fear of falling. Most breeds are carefully set upon the table and then deposited back on the floor, but some larger agile breeds, such as whippets, can be taught to jump on and off by themselves. Unfortunately, picking up a coated breed tends to mess up all the hair that you have so meticulously brushed into place, at exactly the time you want the dog to look its best. You can overcome this problem in lightweight breeds by grasping them by tail and chin, and quickly whisking them up on the table. You can also pick up a long-coated dog up by placing your arm between its rear legs from the rear, and reaching forward so that you are supporting it up to its chest with one arm. Practice the transition from floor to table and back until you can do it smoothly and your dog is not upset.

### Posting

Once posed, take a look at your show dog. Chances are it bears

*To lift a long-coated dog to the table without messing up its coat, place one hand under the dog's body from between its rear legs, supporting its chest and abdomen. Use the other hand to hold the head still.*

very little resemblance to that "look of eagles" you saw in the backyard. Most dogs will "post," that is, lean slightly backwards. Insecure and inexperienced dogs usually post, because they don't naturally stand with their legs stretched behind them. Never pose your dog by

*The cocker spaniel is one of several sporting breeds traditionally posed with the lead off. Note that the handler has draped the lead over her neck so that it is out of the way. She will replace it before placing the dog on the ground.*

pulling the front legs forward in an effort to stretch the dog out; this is guaranteed to result in posting. Any stretching should be done by placing the hind legs backwards, farther back.

There are several ways to get your dog to stop posting, but the first step is to make sure your dog is confident and happy in what it's doing.

## Baiting

Even if you have a happy dog, it has little reason to lean forward. You must give it a reason. The best reason in the eyes of most dogs is a tempting piece of bait enticing them forward. Hold the bait a couple of inches in front of the dog. When the dog leans forward to take the treat, praise, and hand over the treat. Have the dog lean farther forward next time, before rewarding it. If it moves its feet, simply put the bait away, restack it, and try again. Remember to hold the head up so that the neck is not jutting out straight ahead. You want the neck to have an arch, and you can help to create one by baiting the dog forward and slightly down, while holding its head high with the lead.

Dogs that won't bait are more difficult. But remember, for every action there is an equal and opposite reaction. You can try pulling your dog forward until you're blue in the face and never get your dog over its front. The trick is to pull your dog backwards. Grasp the dog by the base of the tail and pull slowly backwards, or push your dog by its chest backwards. Most dogs will respond by leaning forward. Once the dog leans forward, remove your hand slowly and praise. For more extreme results, train by positioning the dog's rear feet on the edge of a curb, so that when you pull backward the feet will slip off the edge unless the dog really pulls itself forward. Of course, never let your dog actually fall off or do anything that might cause it to be injured. Don't have the dog standing on just its toes, which could unduly stress them and possibly cause ligament damage. Eventually your dog will lean forward with just a slight tug on the tail or push on the chest.

If none of the above techniques work, you can push your dog forward somewhat by placing your fingers behind the last rib and pushing forward. This is not particularly comfortable for the dog so it will tend to lean forward. Don't try this with a shy dog, because it will only tend to make it more ill at ease.

## Problems with Feet and Leg Positions

Unless your dog is exceptional, posting won't be its only problem. For feet that don't point straight ahead, you need to overcompensate when posing, twisting the leg and almost screwing it into the ground (taking care, of course, not to hurt the dog!). For dogs that are high in the rear, the rear legs can be posed wider and farther back than usual, at the same time making sure the dog

really leans forward, or you can sometimes subtly press down on the rear. For dogs that are swaybacked, you can tap the dog under its belly, and keep the dog very alert, as well as baiting it forward and down; for dogs that are roachbacked, you can try overstretching the dog or tiring it out before showing, making sure it is not tense, and also baiting it upward.

*Pulling the dog backward can ultimately cause it to lean forward.*

## Collar Placement

You can also affect your dog's expression by the placement of the

*When you quit pulling backwards the dog will be left leaning slightly forward.*

the dog under the chin with your hand. Of course, in a breed in which loose skin or wrinkles are desirable, you may wish to push the excess skin forward so that it hangs around the face. You can also prop the ears up in some dogs by pinching the skin between them together. Tickling behind the ears can also help get them up.

Don't hang your dog by the collar, especially if it's a choke collar. Support its head under the chin with your other hand when the judge is not looking at your dog. When the judge does look, place your fingers between the collar and neck so that the collar cannot become tight on the dog.

## Your Pose

Once you have perfected your dog's pose, what about yours? Your stance will depend upon the

collar. Always keep the collar way up on the neck, in the groove immediately behind the ears. Take any loose skin on the throat and pull it toward you. The collar will hold the skin in place, and this placement will give the neck and chin a sleeker look. You can achieve the same affect by holding

*Which borzoi has the best front? These are three photos of the same dog, posed correctly in the center. On the left, the dog's front is set too wide; note the gap between the chest and the elbows. On the right, the elbows have been twisted inward, causing the front to be too narrow and the feet to turn outward.*

*(Left) For most breeds, including this borzoi, the rear should be set as wide or a little wider than the hips, so that the legs are nearly parallel. (Center) A common mistake is to set the rear too wide, creating an A-frame effect. This makes the rear look weak and causes the dog to appear steep in the croup when viewed from the side. (Right) One way to set the rear is to reach over or behind the dog and pick the leg up at the hock. Note that the handler still keeps the dog's head held up while posing its rear. If she lets go, the dog may move its front feet and she will have to start setting it all over again.*

breed of dog you're showing. You can stand next to the dog, but don't hang over the top of the dog. If you are baiting, you can stand in front of the dog. Or you can kneel next to or in front of the dog. On rare occasions, you can stand behind the dog, but this position gives you virtually no control of the dog and is not generally suggested.

Ball the show lead into your hand so that the loose end isn't flapping around. You can also take the lead and drape it over and behind your neck when stacking, a practice particularly popular when posing a dog on the table. If you find that fiddling with the leash is too distracting, simply let it hang down to the ground.

In some breeds, such as the pointer and setter breeds, the lead is traditionally removed when posing the dog. The handler kneels

*Some possible handler positions.*

*Every dog has a speed at which it looks best, and that speed may be different, depending upon the angle from which the dog is viewed. When moving a dog, always be aware of the viewpoint the judge has of your dog, and adjust your speed accordingly.*

beside the dog, holding the tail extended behind with the left hand, and holding the head under the chin with the right hand. Although you won't usually be expected to pose a class dog (non-champion) off lead (especially in a small class), posing in this manner makes a striking picture. Practice removing and replacing the lead in a coordinated fashion.

### Gaiting

Posing is only half the battle. The other half is moving. Moving the dog is not like taking it for a walk. It is closer to dancing with your dog, a ballet performed for the benefit of the judge.

Remember what the judge is looking for in most breeds: sound movement coming and going, and reach and drive from the side. The judge will also be influenced by showmanship: a dog that is obviously happy and confident, boldly strutting around the ring.

**Going around:** The judge will evaluate movement from two angles. When the request is "Take them around," the dog's side movement will be judged. Practice running in a counterclockwise circle, just as you will do in the ring. When you finish a circle, stop slowly and bait your dog or give it a treat, and then practice posing it. Run in big circles and in little circles, so your dog has practice making left turns in any size ring.

Although you are taught in obedience classes to never let your dog forge ahead of you, for some reason it is the style to have a dog leading its handler around the ring. Few things look worse than a dog being dragged around the ring a few feet behind its handler, but with continued training, dogs tend to go progressively slower, not faster. So as long as you can keep your dog at a trot, let it forge ahead for now.

You are also taught in obedience class to hold the lead in both hands. Never, never do this in the show ring. The lead is held in the left hand only, with the excess balled into the hand. Most people bend their arm at the elbow and hold their hand at about waist level or higher.

Your dog will be trotting on your left side. Place the dog's collar right behind its ears, in that little gap between the head and neck. For small dogs, the lead will come off the top side of the neck, but large dogs may or may not move best that way. Some dogs will hang their heads if you try to pull the head up by the lead. Try rotating the collar so that the leash comes off from under the dog's chin. This will cause many dogs to hold their heads up of their own accord. If your dog repeatedly shakes its head, it's because it finds the lead touching its ears to be irritating. You can try letting the collar fall down on its neck near its withers, but this will only work if you have a dog that is not forging and lunging.

You will eventually need someone to help you choose the best speed for your dog. For now, move the dog so that it is trotting at a swift pace, just below the speed at which it breaks into a canter. If it does break stride, don't snatch it back. Just slow down a bit and start over. If it tries to jump and play, slow down and try a speed at which it will not be so excited. A little goofy exuberance is preferable to sullen compliance.

Don't wave bait in front of your dog as its moves. You want it to look straight ahead, not twist its body in an effort to get to the bait. Some handlers train their dogs by throwing bait ahead of them as they gait. When in the ring, they make the same throwing movements (without actually throwing any bait), in order to keep the dog's attention riveted ahead of it.

**Down and back:** The judge will also evaluate movement directly from the front and rear. The usual request is "Down and back." The key here is the ability to run in a straight line.

I once watched a specialty class where all but two of the 20 entries zigzagged back and forth, intermittently bouncing off their handler and hitting the end of the lead. The two trained dogs were the only ones that moved in a straight line, and they won first and second place. The other dogs acted as though they had never done this before, and perhaps they hadn't. How on earth could the judge be expected to evaluate movement that never traveled in the same direction on consecutive strides?

*Practice makes (almost) perfect!*

You need to practice your down and back enough so that your dog knows what to expect. If it expects you to move in a straight line, it will move in a straight line too. But can you move in a straight line?

*If you have difficulty steering a powerful dog in a straight line, you can enlist the aid of an overhead trot line.*

Remember you'll be doing so while keeping one eye on your dog. Try it without the dog, and practice until you can trot in a dead straight line. Pick a target and run toward it on an imaginary line on the ground if you have a problem.

Only when you can move in a straight line should you ask your dog to join you. If you have a giant breed that is difficult for you to get going straight, attach a second lead to a sturdy overhead run line and practice running back and forth along its length. Take care not to give your dog whiplash when you turn around to start your return trip. Too many people execute a military about turn, giving the dog no warning until it hits the end of the lead and is snapped around. This is no way to build confidence and enthusiasm. As you near the end of your return trip, turn to face your dog and bait it into a semblance of your show pose.

**The best speed:** Every dog has a best speed, which may be different for coming, going, and side movement. For coming and going, you want a speed at which the legs move in a straight line from body to ground, usually converging toward the middle slightly with increasing speed. In general, slower is better. Most, but not all, dogs start moving more erratically and unsoundly with increasing speed. If your dog is great at any speed, move at a medium speed. If your dog is bad at any speed, move fast so the judge has less time to see it!

For side movement, you want to move at a speed that requires the dog to reach out with as long a stride as possible, without having to start moving its legs like pistons. Faster is not necessarily better. A smooth, flowing, almost slow motion gait with a long reach and powerful drive is better than a blur of legs racing around the ring. Too slow, and the dog will not extend enough for the judge to see its full potential. As always, there are exceptions with some breeds.

Decisions about optimal speed can't be made from the end of the lead. A full-length mirror, a knowledgeable friend, or a video camera are all helpful in determining your dog's best speed.

# The Handler's Role

**Movement:** Your own gait and stride is important; after all, you are half of the dance team. With small dogs you can walk at a normal walking pace. With larger dogs, you will need to run, but, unlike a dancer, you don't want to run on your toes. Trotting on your toes makes you bob up and down and look ungainly (and amateurish). The dog show trot is done on your heels, taking long, low, fluid steps. Some people take this to an extreme and look like Groucho Marx. Wrong. Try, instead, to look like you are running in slow motion.

**Your arms and hands:** That pesky right arm is the subject of much confusion among new handlers. The left hand has something to do; it has the lead in it. The right hand has nothing to do while gaiting. But don't:

- hold it in front of the dog's face as though luring it along with bait
- hold it straight out to the side as though balancing on a tight wire
- hold it behind your back or stuck tight to your side as though you were in a straightjacket

The answer is quite simple. Hold it as though you weren't showing a dog. Let it swing naturally at your side, moving as it would normally do as you move. If you have bait in your right hand, don't show it to the dog when on the move. Wait until you prepare to stop before revealing the hidden treasure.

What about handler style and flair? A certain amount is fine, but usually less is best. As soon as your little accents divert the judge's eye from the dog to you, you have

failed. Your style should be that which you should have in every day life: good posture, confident carriage, and a graceful gait. Fancy flourishes can only distract.

## Attitude

Everybody loves a winner—including judges. Judges will rarely put you first simply because they feel sorry for you. Judging is subjective, and if you can walk into the ring exuding confidence, you give the message that at least one person likes your dog, even if it's only you. It's harder to deny a win to someone who is expecting to run to the first place marker than it is to someone who already wants to walk out the gate.

Everyone has an attitude with which they feel most comfortable. Some people smile like crazed lunatics the whole time they are in the ring. Some scowl and glare and almost dare the judge not to place them first! Of course, something in between is probably best. Look

*A common mistake: under the pressure of competition—in this case, for Winners at the National—the handler pushes the dog to go too fast and the dog breaks out of a trot. She should pull back on the lead and slow down before resuming her pace. (Saluki)*

*A happy attitude on the part of the handler will convey itself to the dog, and encourage it to have a happy attitude as well. (Toy poodle)*

pleasant but also serious. This is an area where your own personality will have to shine through. Just let it be a confident side of your personality.

From the moment you step foot into the ring, judging has officially begun. Don't bumble around. Pick a destination (which should correspond to where the judge has placed the dogs in earlier classes) and go there. Set the dog up with a purpose. Don't start setting the front and then switch to the rear and back again. Be decisive.

*Don't* stare at the judge. *Do* look the judge in the face when you are being addressed, and keep an eye on the judge. However, trying to mesmerize the judge is not the answer. It's better to try to use your gaze to direct the judge's attention to your dog. Just as when you see a person staring into the sky you will be inclined to look there as well,

when you look at your dog, others will look there, too. You can use this concept in the ring. Look at your dog, and especially, at your dog's good points. Hopefully, the judge will look, too. Obviously, by the same token, avoid staring at your dog's shortcomings!

When the time comes for the judge to make placements or a cut, then you might look at the judge a little more, using a look of expectant confidence. Convey the message: "I am ready to go to my first place marker."

Of course, your attitude shouldn't really influence a good judge—but a good attitude can't hurt. Besides, a happy attitude will also help give your dog a happy attitude.

# Dress Rehearsals

### Ring Procedure

Now that you have all the components down, it's time to put them together for a dress rehearsal. The best scenario would be to fashion a square ring in your yard and have a friend play judge. Nine times out of ten your time in the ring will go like this:

1. Enter the ring and set your dog up.
2. Trot once around the ring and set your dog up.
3. The judge will examine your dog. You may be asked to show the dog's bite.
4. The judge will ask either for a triangle or for a down and back. Be ready to have your dog self

stack and bait when you get back to the judge.

5. Trot back to the end of the line.
6. Set your dog up.
7. Trot around one more time.
8. Go to first place!

## Match Shows

A better dress rehearsal is a match show, which is an informal show in which everyone is there for practice. This often includes the judges, so never take a win or a loss at a match very seriously. The best way to approach a match is as a learning experience for you and your dog, with no emphasis upon winning or losing. Matches are often held after BIS judging at a regular dog show, or may be held as a separate event. Contact your local kennel club for information about upcoming matches. You can usually enter the day of the match. Dress is casual but neat. Breeds are usually judged in alphabetical order by group, and there are separate competitions for puppies and adults.

# Putting on the Dog

The one thing missing from your dress rehearsal was probably the dress part. Professional handlers handle dogs as their profession; they tend to dress the part. Owner handlers too often look like they're off to slop the hogs, go to a funeral, do the laundry in the creek, or go to a nightclub. If you don't dress as though you are as serious as the professionals are, you probably

*Puppy matches provide a chance to socialize pups and convince them that showing is great fun! (Great Danes)*

won't be perceived to be as ready to win as they are.

**Dress for men:** A dog show is a sporting event, but it is also an event that is steeped in tradition. Dress for men is almost always a sports jacket, nice pants, and a tie. Not a three-piece suit, not jeans, not a short-sleeve shirt. The jacket should be buttoned so that it does not fly around when you are moving, especially if you are showing a large dog that might be repeatedly hit in the face by the jacket. In hot weather it may be permissible to remove your jacket. Take your cue from your judge (if a man). If he keeps his jacket on, you keep yours on.

**Dress for women:** Women have a lot more choices in acceptable attire, but tend to turn up in a lot more unacceptable outfits. A dress or skirt is most popular, but a nice pants suit is totally acceptable and especially sensible when showing toy breeds or any breed requiring a great deal of bending and kneeling. Stories abound of judges who allegedly award the wins to scantily clad women, but such judges are not very common (besides, their wives are usually sitting ringside!). Don't wear a dress so short or a top so low-cut that you can't bend over without giving ringside a view. Wraparound skirts have a tendency to become unwrapped around when showing at a fast run or on a windy day. Long, full skirts have a tendency to billow in front of the dog at windy outdoor shows, partially obscuring the judge's view of the dog's movement. Poor fitting slips and even underpants have been known to fall down when the handler was running around the ring, providing quite an embarrassing spectacle! When in doubt, a semicasual jacket and skirt can't go wrong.

**Color:** Color is as important as style. Your black dog with a perfect outline will be lost if you wear a black outfit. Of course, your black dog with the horrible topline might do well to have that topline blend into your clothing. Most people try to wear a color that will contrast with the color of the dog. Like people, dogs have colors in which they look their best. Spotted dogs are a challenge. Try to wear a color that is not on the dog, to avoid the problem of only parts of the dog blending into your outfit. Solid colors usually look best with multicolored dogs.

**Pockets:** The best outfits have pockets in which combs, squeaky toys, or bait can be carried. In the absence of pockets, bait pouches (available from some dog show vendors) can be attached to a belt.

**Jewelry:** Jewelry should not clank and rattle when you trot, nor should it hit the dog in the head when you bend over. Don't carry loose change in your pockets, which will make a racket when you run.

**Shoes:** Dog show exhibitors will never be known for their fashion savvy when it comes to shoes. Flat shoes with rubber nonskid soles are a must. This is one of the only sporting events in existence in which the contestants may be running at full speed wearing a suit or dress. Unless you have a slow moving breed, you will need to really shop for your shoes. This doesn't mean that you must wear running shoes. Giant running shoes look really out of place with a dress or a suit and are seldom worn by professionals. A variety of semifashionable shoes are available that will fit the bill. A spare pair of rain shoes should be in your travel bag.

In choosing an outfit, always remember: You are showing the dog, not yourself. Decorating yourself like a Christmas tree will probably not provide the best backdrop for your dog; anything you wear that is distracting can only draw attention away from your dog, not to it.

I have had friends who have spent fabulous sums on new clothes for the next show. They shop and shop for just the right dress, go to the show and lose, and decide they need a better outfit for the next show. A great outfit will never make you win. It is a backdrop for your dog and a signal of respect for the event and is only one of many ingredients in a winning team.

# Chapter Six

# Ready, Set, Show!

It's a big step from sitting at home watching the Westminster Dog Show on television with your future champion in your lap to being one of the exhibitors actually floating around the ring at Madison Square Garden. But every trip around the ring starts with a single step, and your first step is to find that ring.

You can find upcoming dog shows by joining your local kennel club, or by subscribing to the *AKC Gazette* or to *Dog World*. Any serious exhibitor should start with a subscription to the *AKC Gazette*, which includes articles on all facets of dogs, AKC updates, and a listing of all upcoming judging panels. The April issue contains yearly show statistics and should be kept for year-long reference. The separate *Show Awards* lists the results of all AKC shows and other events, and will provide you with the thrill of seeing your dog's name in teeny print if it should win a ribbon. (For the address and phone number of the *AKC Gazette*, see page 141.)

The *AKC Official Rules and Regulations for Dog Shows* should accompany you to every dog showing event. It provides a complete listing of the rules that concern the dog show exhibitor and is available from the AKC and at any dog show.

You will also want to be placed on the mailing lists of the AKC show superintendents in your area (see Useful Addresses, page 139) so that your mailbox will be jammed with premium lists for shows in locales that you would never have considered local. But you can't just show up at a show and expect to enter your dog. With thousands of dogs entered in a single show, a considerable amount of preparation is involved from show organizers after entries are received. This is why entries for a regular AKC dog show close approximately two and half weeks before the show.

The premium list will tell you the exact closing date, show location, whether it will be held indoors or outdoors, who the judges will be, any special classes or class divisions, any special rules, and what (if any) prizes are offered. If you are a procrastinator some superintendents will allow you to phone or fax your entries for an added fee. But whatever way you send them, be aware of one thing: When it says entries close at noon on Wednesday, they really do!

There are instructions on the entry form in the premium list that will help you to fill it out. Double-check everything, and call the superintendent if you have any questions. The hardest blank to fill in is the one for which you must decide which class to enter.

# The Right Class

The AKC rules for dog shows explain in great detail the requirements for each class but they don't explain why you might prefer to enter one class over another. In a perfect world, you would have an equal chance of winning points from any class. The dog show world is not perfect.

Enter only one class, even though you might be eligible for more. If you are defeated in any class, you won't be eligible to compete in the Winners class. Besides, only rank novices enter more than one, with the exception of non-regular classes offered at specialty shows.

- **Puppy:** This is usually an easy choice. If you have a puppy between the age of six and twelve months, enter Puppy class; however, there are some reasons to occasionally not enter Puppy class. If your puppy is abnormally large for its age, it may tower over the other pups and look out of place, causing the judge to wonder if it will be oversize later. Some judges will not put up a puppy for Winners,

so if your pup is extremely mature for its age, you may decide to go for broke and enter an adult class in an attempt to win the points. An extremely sound, well put-together puppy that is still obviously a puppy cannot help but get the judges' attention if it is entered in Open; it sends the message to the judge that you know this pup is good enough to compete with adults and that you have a lot of confidence in it.

Still, the general rule is that for most puppies, at most shows, you should enter the Puppy class. You will have plenty of time to get serious later and, after all, puppies should be allowed to be puppies.

Be sure to check whether this class is divided by age and that you enter the correct age division. In fact, it's a good idea to always enter as though the class were divided. If you do enter the wrong age division, you can correct it the day of the show and compete in the correct class. If you don't correct it, your awards will be disallowed.

- **12–18 month:** The decision whether to enter this class is far less clear-cut. In most breeds, especially at a large show or specialty, you should take advantage of this class if your dog is eligible. But in a breed or at a show in which there will be few entries anyway, you may wish to enter a class with more competition.

Again, if your dog is still puppyish, by all means enter it in the class that explains why it is puppyish.

- **Novice:** The requirements for the Novice class are that a dog has never won a blue ribbon in an Open or Bred by Exhibitor class, or has won no more than three firsts in Puppy or Novice classes. Because most people don't think this is a good way to convince a judge that their dog is worthy of winning points, this class is seldom well populated at most shows. Still, the Novice class is an excellent choice at large shows or specialty shows; it is better to place first in Novice than nothing in Open, and while uncommon, dogs can win the points from the Novice class.

- **Bred by Exhibitor:** This class requires that the dog be owned by the person or spouse of the person who bred the dog, and that the dog be handled by the breeder or by a member of the breeder's family (spouse, parent, child, or sibling). Because this class is often used by experienced breeders to showcase their best stock, it usually has some of the toughest competition, and is not recommended for newcomers. Besides, as a newcomer, you shouldn't have a dog eligible for this class.

- **American-Bred:** In the old days, dogs imported from England cleaned up at the shows. In order to encourage the exhibition of dogs "made in the U.S.A.," the American-Bred class was created. Competition was keen and shows even had awards up to Best American-Bred in Show. Although the competition is less keen these days, the American-Bred class is still alive and well, and available to any dog whelped in the United States.

  In breeds with overwhelming Open classes, especially breeds where all of the dogs look somewhat alike, some people enter American-Bred so that they won't be lost in a sea of dogs. They can then take their chances on a more one-on-one competition in the Winners class. In breeds with smaller entries, however, American-Bred has a tendency to be equated with "not quite ready for prime-time."

- **Open:** Open is the class for the serious contenders. If winning the points is your goal, and at some point it will be, and if your dog is ready to contend, then this is the class for you. Even for the newcomer, Open can be a good choice. Many beginners choose a class with less competition in the belief that it will be easier to show in. It is not. A small class gives you no time to think, relax, or prepare. In a one-dog class you are the center of attention, and when you're just starting out and bumbling around, that's not always so good. In a two-dog class you are just as hurried, and even a three-dog class can be tough. The easiest classes to show in are those with four or more dogs, and Open tends to be the largest class. Keep in mind, however, that if your dog is in Open, the judge will expect it to be mature and trained, and will be far less forgiving of puppy shenanigans. Also, be forewarned that your chances of winning any ribbon at all are slimmest in this class because the competition is tougher.

In some breeds the Open classes may be divided, sometimes on the basis of color, coat type, height, or weight. In such breeds it's a good idea to always include the proper division on your entry form, even if the class isn't divided. If the class is divided and you haven't indicated the proper division, your entry will be rejected.

- **Best of Breed:** Only dogs that have already met the requirements to be designated an AKC Champion are eligible for this class. Champions can also be entered in Open, but no one ever does so. Best of Breed competition is also referred to as "specials" class, and dogs entered in this class are called "specials."

**Non-regular classes:** At specialty shows there may be special classes such as veteran, stud dog, brood bitch, or brace, the requirements of which will be described in the premium list. There may also be a Sweepstakes offered, judged by a different judge, and usually limited to puppies and young adults (but occasionally also for elderly dogs). If you have a dog eligible for Sweepstakes, by all means enter it so that you will have an extra chance to practice, and perhaps even win!

## Breeds and Varieties

A few breeds are divided into "sub-breeds," or varieties. The varieties do not compete against each other except at specialty shows. If you do not indicate the proper variety on your entry form, your entry will be rejected.

The breeds that are divided into varieties are shown on page 63.

# Dog Show Ins and Outs

If possible, choose an outdoor show for your dog's show debut. Indoor shows are crowded and loud, and far too confusing for a novice dog. The grooming sections are madhouses, full of barking dogs and chattering people. In addition, most indoor shows have fairly slippery flooring. Inside the rings, rubber matting is used, but it can be difficult to keep an untrained dog centered on the mat. Outside the rings, no such matting is present, and large breeds, especially, can slip and slide on the way to the ring.

## Outdoor Shows

Outdoor shows are easier for most dogs to accept. The footing is usually grass, and dogs can get

## Breeds and Varieties

### Beagles
13 inch (33 cm) (under 13 inches
   in height)
15 inch (38 cm) (over 13 inches
   but under 15 inches in height)

### Bull terriers
Colored
White

### Chihuahuas
Long coat
Smooth coat

### Cocker spaniels
Black (and black and tan)
Parti-color (spotted)
ASCOB (any solid color other
   than black)

### Collies
Rough
Smooth

### Dachshunds
Longhaired
Smooth
Wirehaired

### English toy spaniels
Blenheim and Prince Charles
King Charles and Ruby

### Manchester terriers
Standard (over 12 pounds [54 kg]
   not exceeding 22 pounds
   [9.9 kg])
Toy (not exceeding 12 pounds
   [5.4 kg])

### Poodles
Standard (over 15 inches [38 cm])
Miniature (over 10 inches
   [25.4 cm] not exceeding 15
   inches [38 cm])
Toy (not exceeding 10 inches
   [25.4 cm])

good traction. The exception are some toy dogs that are never exercised on grass, and do not like it one bit. At outdoor shows you can find wide open spaces and get away from other dogs and people. In fact, most dogs will find it enjoyable to be on a walk in the park with you. Weather, of course, can be unpredictable. Don't expect judging to stop because of a sudden deluge or because the rings are under water. Unless you hear an announcement to the contrary (or with the possible exception of a tornado), assume the show is continuing on schedule. Always bring rain gear for you and your dog. With the exception of giant breeds, most dogs are carried through the muck so that they arrive ringside in immaculate condition. Doggy boots are handy when you can't carry your dog. Even plastic bags affixed with rubber bands can do in a fix. Depending on coat type, a last minute application of cornstarch, which is then thoroughly brushed out, can help to dry wet and muddy feet.

Outdoor shows can be intensely hot so bring a cooler with ice water to keep ringside. Fill a spritzer bottle with the cool water and spray some in the dog's mouth, and anywhere on its body that will not mess up its coat. You can also lay a damp cold towel over your dog's back. Stay under the tent shade as much as possible, or bring your own sunshade. When in the ring and not under the tent, shield your dog from the sun with your own shadow except when posing for the judge.

## Benched Shows

In the good old days, all dog shows were "benched," meaning that dogs were placed on a bench, or small platform, to be on display for the public for the entire day. Win or lose, every dog had to be at the show from early in the morning until late in the afternoon. Not only were benched shows a wonderful forum for the world of purebred dogs, but they afforded exhibitors ample opportunity to talk to each other and exchange ideas about the breed. Benched shows are now a rarity. They are hard on both exhibitor and dog, and are not advisable for your pup's first experience.

# It's About Time

About a week before the big event, a judging schedule should appear in your mailbox. The judging schedule will tell you how to get to the show (sort of), and more impor-

tant, when your breed will be judged. First look at the top of the schedule. You may see a statement that one or more judges are being substituted. If this happens with your judge—and eventually it will—you can get a refund for that day by writing the superintendent before the show starts and requesting to withdraw your entry. However, until you get to know one judge from another, you might as well take your chances with the new one.

Look in the breed index to find out the ring in which your breed will be judged. Then look under the listing for that ring. It might look something like this:

**Ring 2**
8:30 A.M.
23 Italian Greyhounds 6–14–3–1
15 Chihuahuas (Smooth Coat)
  3–10–1–1

10:00 A.M.
3 Manchester Terriers (Toy)
  1–1–0–1
4 Brussels Griffons 1–1–1–1
10 Maltese 3–6–1–0

**Translation:** A total of 23 Italian greyhounds are entered. The four numbers following the breed name break down the 23 entries as follows:

6 nonchampion dogs
14 nonchampion bitches
3 champion dogs
1 champion bitch

When you begin your quest for majors, this listing will become extremely important for you. If there are not enough nonchampions entered to make a major, it may not be worth your time to travel to the show. For now, the number is not so important just as long as one of them is yours.

The assigned times are the earliest times at which a breed can be judged, but your actual show time might be as much as an hour later. Most schedules are based upon an average judging speed of about 25 dogs per hour. This means that if you have a Chihuahua scheduled at 8:30, you'll more likely not enter the ring until nearly 9:30. You won't want to cut it that close, of course, because there could be absentees that could affect the number. For example, although seven dogs are scheduled before the Maltese, notice that for four of those dogs (the single-entry nonchampion dogs) there are no points available unless they perform the unlikely feat of beating the champions. Chances are very good that their owners decided to stay home and save their money, so count on at least some (or most) of these dogs being absent. Also, although it is rare, it is entirely possible that the order of breed judging within that time slot can be rearranged, so that the Maltese might unexpectedly be judged first.

Along with the schedule you will receive a confirmation ticket indicating your armband number. Some fancier shows will require this

*The excitement mounts as showtime approaches. Try to channel any nervous energy into happy times for your dog, rather than tense times. (West Highland white terrier)*

in order to admit you to the building without charging an admission fee, so *don't lose it!*

## Attack of the Butterflies

If you're starting to feel a little nervous—in fact, downright queasy—don't think you're unusual. For an event that really is very insignificant in the scheme of life, dog shows cause an inordinate amount of digestive unease, even in seasoned professionals. It does get better, but the butterflies mainly signal that the event is important to you and that there are many unknowns involved. The best way to quiet them is to either care less about the outcome (which defeats the whole purpose) or to do away with as many unknowns as possible. In other words, be prepared.

*These Chihuahuas can relax or romp in their exercise pen, complete with shade tarps, vinyl ground mat, chew toys, and water bowl.*

## Dog Stuff

- leash and collar
- show lead
- all grooming supplies
- grooming towel
- grooming table (optional, depending on breed)
- water
- bowls
- dog food
- diarrhea medication
- first aid kit
- paper towels
- shade
- exercise pen (optional)
- poop scoop or plastic baggies
- cage
- bait

In popular dog lore little Timmy washes his dog in the river, hikes to the show miles away (perhaps saving a baby and fighting a grizzly bear on the way), arrives at the show, finds a rope to use as a leash, and wins a blue ribbon. In the real world, show dogs may be anointed with special hair potions, driven to the show in air-conditioned motor homes, and carried ringside on velvet pads. Although much of the paraphernalia heaped on show dogs has little effect on whether or not they win, it tends to give their owners something to do and tote and helps make them feel they've done what they can. So your first assignment is to find a way to pack all of the "essentials" so that you don't have to rent a trailer to carry them (see the boxed lists on this page).

## People Stuff

- food and drink
- judging schedule with directions
- map
- money
- chairs
- show outfit
- extra show clothes
- after-show clothes
- umbrella

# The Grand Tour

Always leave home ridiculously early. Budget time for the extra 50 trips for last-minute essentials, and for finding your dog who is suddenly stuck under the bed or, if the dog show gods are really frowning upon you, is in the yard rolling in something dead (it's happened to me!). Budget time for cleaning up a carsick dog. Budget time for getting lost. One of the particular joys of dog shows is the chance to explore exotic locales and prominent land-marks such as livestock barns on the fairgrounds of obscure counties. An added bonus is the opportunity to explore uncharted roads and meet a multitude of gas station attendants in your attempts to follow someone's bizarre sense of direction to the showgrounds. Keep an eye out for vans or motor homes with doggy bumper stickers and follow them when you're hopelessly lost. Maybe they've been there before!

## Not So Fast...

As your destination finally looms in the distance, don't be lulled into a false sense of security, because there is a yet greater challenge ahead: the parking space. You might think that if you get to the show first thing in the morning you will have a front row space. But those spaces were taken as soon as the gates opened the day before by dog show zealots who live from dog show to dog show, and have motor homes the size of nuclear submarines accompanied by an army of orange cones saving spaces for their friends. Your space will be at the farthest reaches of the lot, next to the motor home with the deafening and smothering generator that is unfortu-nately neither loud enough nor smelly enough to drown out the 20 dogs they have stuck in X-pens all day. No matter, you're not planning to spend the day in the parking lot; you're here to go to the show!

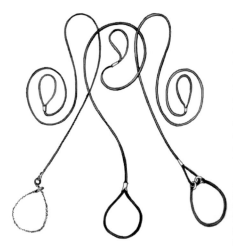

*Types of show leads and collars:*
*Left: Choke collar, made of either a fine chain or nylon, combined with a fine lead, with or without a snap.*
*Center: "Resco" type, an adjustable, non-choking one piece lead.*
*Right: Martingale, a one piece lead that allows a limited extent of tightening on the neck.*

Once parked, it's a good idea to send a scouting party to the actual show to locate your ring and per-haps pick up your armband. You might send along some of your ringside essentials:

- comb and/or brush
- liver and/or squeaky mouse
- chair
- cushion or blanket for dog
- small towel
- spritzer bottle (outdoor shows)
- judging schedule
- cold drinks

## Your Home Away from Home

Depending on the weather and your own facilities, you may wish to set up camp inside the building or under the grooming tent, allowing your dog to snooze in its cage until showtime. Space in either can be so scarce that unless you arrive first thing in the morning, or even the night before, you may not find an available niche. In hot weather this can present a real dilemma. If it is

*Two for the show! Not only does a cage provide protection while riding, but allows for better ventilation once at the show. (Cardigan Welsh corgi)*

for just a second and be waylaid by someone you know and forget how hot it is outside. At every summer show an announcement is made for somebody to get to their car because their dog is in trouble. What a sad commentary at an event that should be displaying the utmost in responsible dog ownership.

## Places to Visit

In addition to your ring, there are a few more places to find inside the show. One is the catalog sales table, where you can buy a catalog that lists the vital statistics of every dog in the show. It is here that you will finally find out the entries in each class. Unless you enjoy spending money there is no need to buy a catalog every day on a multi-show weekend in which all of the dogs are the same. In fact, if the entry is small, you can skip buying a catalog at all by perusing the superintendent's catalog. The superintendent's table is another important landmark. At the superintendent's table all of the official happenings of the show take place. Any problems or questions you have, they can fix or deal with. And on the table is usually a catalog marked "Look at but do not take." This is a catalog for exhibitors to examine who don't wish to buy a catalog. Although at first you'll almost certainly want your own catalog, eventually they present a fire hazard in the home and you may prefer to just take a peek or even offer to buy the pages for your breed out of somebody else's catalog.

an indoor show, you can put your dog on lead and sit ringside with it all day, but this seldom does wonders for its showmanship when its turn finally comes. You can try to find shade and sit with your dog in the car. This is when a battery-driven fan (or better, a small generator) and a reflective blanket for the windshield come in handy. *Never leave your dog closed up in your vehicle.* It's too easy to run inside

*"When is it going to be our turn?" If you anticipate a long wait, bring something comfortable on which your dog can relax—in this case, a lap! (Whippet)*

## People to See

While on the tour be sure to go to your ring and pick up your armband. Ask the steward (when he or she is not occupied with the judge) for "Maltese puppy dog number 5," for example. Rip little notches in the armband so it won't slip out from under the rubber band (which can usually be found in a little bag next to the steward's table) you have placed around your upper left arm. Once in a rare while there will be some clerical matter that you must clear up with the superintendent, so this is another reason not to leave things to the last moment. You must get your armband every day, even if you have a dashboard full of "number 5" armbands. This is how the steward knows your dog is present.

What to do if:

- you don't get a premium list for a show you wish to attend: If there is time, call the appropriate superintendent and request one. Otherwise, take an official AKC entry form for another show, mark through the show name and date, and write by hand the exact name and date, including year, of the show you wish to enter.
- you've waited to the last minute to enter and don't know if your entries will make it on time: You

can usually phone or fax your entries in for an additional fee, or overnight deliver them to a separate address. The premium list will describe these options.

- your judging schedule hasn't arrived by five days before the show: Call the superintendent and get confirmation and directions.
- you forget your entry confirmation: Unless it's a benched show, don't worry; they are virtually never asked for. When you pick up your armband ask the steward to look in the catalog and your dog's number should be listed by its name.
- you change your mind about entering a show: You can cancel and get a refund as long your cancellation reaches the superintendent by the closing date.

*The number one consideration at an outdoor show is comfort, especially of the dog. Not only can heat sap the energy from a dog and convince it that dog shows aren't any fun, but the combination of heat and excitement can prove dangerous. This young Saint Bernard seems to be taking it all in stride, thanks to its considerate owners!*

## Chapter Seven
# It's Showtime!

As you stand ringside clutching your armband and watching the ballet of dogs and handlers around you, you may wonder what on earth you've gotten yourself into and say, "Never again!" It's only natural to have a little stage fright but most people have an inflated idea of how much attention onlookers will be paying them. Most spectators are far too busy chatting or worrying about their own dogs to be studying any goofy moves you might be making inside the ring. And any decent judge is there to judge the dog, not the handler.

Your competition will also be ringside. Some friendly exhibitors may ask about your dog, and even give you some pointers. If they are increasing your nervousness, just tell them you need to be alone with your dog but that you hope to talk to them after you show. Don't be intimidated because they suddenly tell you your dog's tail is too low or too high and you must do such and such to hide it. Worry about that your next show. Your competition's dogs may suddenly look invincible, and they may very well be nice but they may also have their own bag of faults of which their handlers are

acutely aware, so don't defeat yourself before you even enter the ring. Your job at this point is to show your dog the way you've practiced. If you do that, and your dog is good, eventually you will prevail. So calm down, and try to approach this as a training exercise.

## The Last Detail

It never fails that as you do your last minute grooming you will see a hair that the scissors missed. If it makes you feel good to snip it off, go ahead; but in reality, one long hair or one long whisker never made a dog lose. Don't upset the dog by going after these stragglers; they're the least of your worries now!

### When to Head Ringside

The question of when to head ringside is not so simple as it sounds. It depends upon your dog's personality, the weather, and of course, just when your breed is scheduled to be judged. If your dog is inexperienced, shy, or overly rambunctious, you will want to get ringside very early, but as your dog gains experience, or if it tends to be lethargic or dull, you will want to whisk it ringside at the last possible moment. Most newcomers err on the side of getting their dogs ringside too early rather than too late. Your ideal goal is to have your dog acclimated enough so that it is confident and energetic, yet under control when it enters the ring. The hotter the weather the faster your dog will loose energy and wilt, and the closer you will want to cut your margin.

## Last Chance

Make sure your dog has defecated. Your dog is very likely as nervous as you are, and nervous dogs tend to defecate in the ring. If possible, walk your dog back outside or away from the ring and give it a second chance to relieve itself. For dogs that refuse to defecate away from home, you can try inserting a paper match about halfway into the anus; the sensation will often cause the dog to have a bowel movement. If that doesn't work, don't forget to remove the match before going into the ring!

## Toy Dogs

Take toy dogs to the ring in their small cage for their safety as well as comfort. Carry your toy dog to the ring gate so it isn't intimidated or endangered by walking through a land of giants.

**Important:** Always be careful when holding or walking a toy dog around large dogs, who may see the tiny toy as prey. Many large-dog owners are not as careful as

they should be. Never take a chance with your small dog.

## Larger Dogs

Bring a pad for your larger dog to lie on if you might be waiting ringside for awhile, unless yours is a "tough" breed and you don't want it to look like a sissy! Hold your dog's lead tightly; dogs in strange places can act unpredictably.

## A Ringside Seat

Once ringside, find a spot away from the gate and out of the way. The best vantage point is on the diagonal opposite the judge.

Watch the judge's pattern. Most judges use the same procedure all day long and expect you to be familiar with it by the time you enter the ring. Are the dogs lined up in the ring in catalog order? Where do they stand when they get into the ring? Do they trot around or pose first? Does the judge go over all of the dogs at once or one at a time? Does he or she move them in a triangle or down and back? Mentally

*Study the judge's ring procedure before you get in the ring. It looks like this handler has even taught his dogs to study the pattern! (English setters)*

*The dog between the Dalmatian and the black and tan coon hound in this Junior Showmanship class would not be visible to the judge from this angle, because the dogs on both sides of it are set out farther. Don't allow your dog to be lost in the crowd.*

rehearse what you will do in the ring. Remember your training sessions. Practice setting your dog up one last time. Keep your dog happy. As your class nears, get close to the gate so you don't have to make a mad dash through a crowd of dogs. Listen for your class to be called. Let the dogs from the previous class get out of the ring before trying to get in. If your dog meets one of the dogs leaving the ring face to face, it could result in a bite or in your dog becoming suddenly intimidated at the very moment you want it to be brimming with confidence. Always use the ring gate; *never* step over the ring.

## Class Order

All nonchampion males are shown first, in the following order: Puppy 6–9; Puppy 9–12; 12–18; Novice; Bred by Exhibitor; American-Bred; and Open; followed by Winners and Reserve Winners dog. The same classes are then held for bitches. Champions are not shown until the final class, Best of Breed.

## Class Position

If the judge is not calling the dogs in catalog order, you may be able to choose your position within the class. As a newcomer, try to avoid being either first or last. Both of these positions require you to hurry to stack your dog; however, shy dogs are often scared by dogs behind them, so in this case you may have to try to go last in line. If you tell the other exhibitors of your desire to go in last, they will usually comply.

In a large class, the judge will spend most of the time in the middle of the ring, so that the rears of the dogs at the front of the line and the fronts of the dogs at the end of the line are most easily seen. This means that if your dog has a bad rear, you should try to be near the end of the line, so that the judge would have to walk way to that side of the ring to get a good look at it. A bad front or ugly head goes to the front of the line. A bad profile should go anywhere but the middle of the line. You won't hide any fault entirely, but at least you won't be constantly reminding the judge of it.

As you gain more experience, you will recognize who the main contenders are in your class. Your initial impulse is to stay away from them in line so that your dog won't be overshadowed by them. Wrong!

If you have a choice, get next to the dog favored to win. You want the judge to compare your dogs side by side and see that yours is better. If yours isn't really better, it won't matter where you are in the ring.

# Let the Show Begin!

The moment your dog's feet enter the ring the show has begun. Take a deep breath and walk confidently to your place with your dog's head held high. Set your dog up but be ready to move when the judge tells you to. Remember to be decisive in your actions; if you start to set the front up, finish it before heading to the rear. At the same time, don't become so involved in setting your dog that you are oblivious to the judge's instructions. You must keep one eye on your dog and one eye on the judge at all times.

## Where to Pose Your Dog

At an indoor show, pose your dog facing to your right with its left feet almost to the inner edge of the mat. For some reason everyone seems to think that sticking a dog a little closer to the judge will cause the judge to notice it more, so if you're not right at the edge you're likely to be hidden behind other dogs. Leave a reasonable distance between your dog and the one in front of you; a couple of feet is usually good. When outdoors, set up in line with the dog ahead of you. Pay attention to bumps and hills that could distort your dog's stance, and reposition your dog if need be in order to avoid them.

Avoid setting up behind a tent pole, examination table, or anything that could block the judge's view of your dog. In a large class the line may extend beyond just one side of the ring. If you find yourself at a corner, you must be extra careful that you are not hidden from the judge's view by the two dogs on either side of you (see diagram).

Double-check your dog's stack before you start standing there with a confident grin on your face while your dog has subtly crossed its

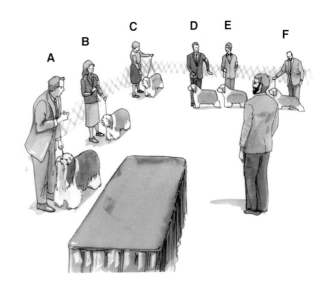

*When setting up in the ring, take care not to make the mistake of handler A, who is hidden from the judge by the examination table, handler C, who is partially hidden because the dog is placed too far into the corner, or handler D, who has allowed himself to be crowded from behind (he needs to ask handler E to back up).*

front feet, gotten its lip hung up on its canine tooth, and has a big tentacle of drool hanging from its mouth. Incidentally, nervous dogs tend to drool, so you might want to have a cloth handy, especially if your dog is hot or has pendulous lips. A tiny squirt of lemon juice can also cut the drool.

## Ringside Help

A ringside friend can be an asset, so glance at him or her for a critique every once in a while. Your friend can help with subtle advice, or by carrying you a brush or water spritzer, by handling a mussed coat, but cannot step foot into the ring nor call the dog to get its attention. So-called "double-handling" is against the rules, although certain breeds, most notably German shepherd dogs, are known for being double-handled. If your friend just happens to be sitting ringside with a bitch in heat, and your male alerts to her, fine, but your friend can't run from one side of the ring to the other waving her arms so that your dog never takes its eyes off of her.

## First Impressions

The judge may or may not give the entire class a quick look. Remember that first impressions are very important. Most judges will then move the entire class one or two times around the ring. If you are the first in line, it's a good idea to check that the other handlers are ready, and even ask the handler behind you if he or she is ready. The judge wants to compare side movement, and can't easily do that if your dog has already jetted around the ring ahead of the others.

## "Take Them All Around"

When moving as a group with the other dogs, be sure to give the dog in front of you ample room so that you don't run up on its rear. Also be aware of when that dog stops. Accidents have occurred when a handler was too busy looking at his or her own dog and rear-ended the dog or handler ahead who had stopped. If the dog in front of you is such a slug that your dog can't move at its best speed, make a note to give it a bigger head start next time, and slow down when you are behind the judge, so that the

*The judge will often walk behind the line of dogs, asking his favorites to move down and back once more. Note how this handler has positioned himself so that the judge has a clear view of his dog at all times. (Great Dane)*

gap has widened by the time you are in front of the judge. Then speed up so that your dog is at its best gait when you are in front of the judge. The only time you can pass another dog is if that dog has had to stop for some reason. Beware of slippery floors indoors, and of tent stakes outdoors.

## While Waiting Your Turn

After moving the class, most judges will examine each dog individually. In a large class, unless you are first or second in line, allow your dog to relax while the other entrants are being examined. Some judges will glance back at all of the dogs periodically, so keep your dog looking good at the same time. This is when baiting comes in handy. If your dog just has to look hangdog, at least shield it from the judge with your body, hide behind another dog, or let it sit or even lie down. Set your dog up again when the judge goes over the dog ahead of you, after your dog has just moved and is last in line, and of course after all the dogs have been examined and the judge is looking at the entire class.

Some exhibitors think that now is the time to strike up a conversation with the other exhibitors, but you've put too much effort into this outing to give your dog anything less than 100 percent of your attention. Perhaps these exhibitors are so experienced they can keep their dog looking good while they talk, perhaps they know they can't even if

*In a large class you won't want to keep your dog posed throughout, but you will want to keep it looking good in case the judge glances your way. (Afghan hound)*

they try, perhaps they are simply not very good handlers themselves and don't know any better, or perhaps they are doing it on purpose just to keep you distracted. In any case, be polite, and either tell them you'd love to talk after judging, or

*The judge will usually begin the examination by evaluating the dog's expression. (Samoyed)*

*Smaller dogs are examined on a table. By baiting the dog downward, this handler accentuates the gracefully arched neckline desired in many breeds. (Whippet)*

simply turn all of your attention to your dog to discourage any further conversation. You have all day to talk, but only a couple of minutes in the ring.

### It's Your Turn

When the dog ahead of you begins to move, place your dog in its position (or on the examining table for a small breed) and pose it

*In breeds in which the head is framed by a ruff, baiting the head slightly upward accentuates the framing. (Shetland sheepdog)*

quickly. As the judge comes to examine your dog individually you should have it stacked to perfection, with special attention to getting the front and rear straight. Often, dogs that were happy and baiting throughout quit now that the pressure is on. Try to relax and convince the dog you are not as nervous as you really are. Tickling the ear base can sometimes help bring ears forward when the dog won't alert on its own.

Don't give the dog a hunk of bait before the judge goes to examine the bite; judges won't appreciate trying to do so as the dog munches away. Some judges will ask you to show the bite. Simply lift the lips and show the area from the fangs forward, unless yours is a breed in which the standard specifically calls for full dentition. In that case, you will want to also show the premolars. In a few breeds, the judge will open the dog's mouth to peer at its molars or tongue color.

Many dogs will lean away from the judge or break their stack to lick the judge. Although neither situation is ideal, it's not necessarily disastrous. Most judges will let you set up again and are good enough that they can see the merits of a dog in any position.

### Moving Your Dog

After the examination keep your dog posed; judges often want to take another look before moving the dog. Now the judge will move your dog. Few things annoy judges more than moving 50 dogs down and back and then having a handler arrive who looks at them vacuously and asks to have the directions to be repeated. Most judges will want a simple "down and back." This is easier at an indoor show with mats because you can center your dog on the mat and have it take a reasonably straight route. However, without a mat you need to take a bearing on an object across the ring, and then lower your gaze and draw an imaginary line along the ground that you will try to follow. Before this you will have walked your dog in front of the judge.

**The courtesy turn:** Many people believe in something called the *courtesy turn*, in which the dog and handler walk in front of the judge and first perform a 270 degree pirouette before starting. For some reason this is supposed to start the dog out straight, but it always seems instead to have the effect of dizzying the dog and annoying the judge. Use a courtesy turn if you would otherwise not start in a straight line, but don't think you have to use one if you are already in correct position.

**Don't rush.** Nervous handlers think they must obey the judge's instructions within a nanosecond, and as a result all of their wonderful plans tend to be forgotten. You've paid a high entry fee considering the time you are in the ring. Get your money's worth. Don't move your dog until you're ready. Get the collar in position. Get the dog's

*"Down and Back": You may or may not perform a "courtesy turn" before beginning. Then go straight away from the judge. At the far side of the ring turn around slowly with the dog on the outside of the turn, unless it is a toy breed, which can be on the inside of the turn. Stop about three to five feet (1–2 m) in front of the judge and have the dog stand itself.*

attention. Get your own wits about you and think about what you're doing. Of course you can't just stand there and look blank while time ticks away, but five seconds is not unreasonable.

**The down and back:** Move your dog at the speed you have already determined is its best. When you get to the far side of the ring, warn your dog that you are now stopping and turning. Even experienced handlers are often guilty of executing military about turns while their dogs

*"Triangle": The initial "courtesy turn" is optional. Follow the outer perimeter of the ring with the dog to the inside of the ring. After the first two legs, make an acute left turn and follow the diagonal back to the judge. With large breeds, it is easier to make this acute turn by making a 270 degree turn to the outside (actually a "courtesy turn") so that you don't trip over the dog.*

Baiting is usually appropriate and helpful at this time. If you have a breed in which the ears should be pricked, squeak a toy or toss a bit of bait (taking care not to hit the judge or anyone else and to pick up the bait before moving again).

**The triangle:** The judge may ask you to move in a triangle. The first leg of the triangle is on the mat along the side of the ring, moving counterclockwise. The judge will evaluate the dog's rear movement at this time. The second leg is along the side of the ring opposite the judge. Here the judge evaluates side movement, and most people will move their dogs at a faster pace. The final leg requires a sharp left turn to approach the judge along the diagonal ring mat so that front movement can be evaluated. It is easier to make this sharp turn with a large dog by executing the courtesy turn rather than a left turn (see diagram). The remainder of this leg is performed the same way as the last half of the down and back.

**The "L":** A very few judges will ask for an "L." This is done by going straight away from the judge, turning left and following the mat to the far side of the ring just as though you were doing the first two legs of a triangle. Now for the tricky part—retracing your steps back to the judge. If you simply turn around, all the judge will see is your movement, because you will be between the judge and the dog. Therefore, you need to have your dog gait on your right side for the return side-move-

hit the end of the lead and are snapped around by their neck as though on some perverted carnival ride. Is it any wonder these dogs tire of shows or look hesitant on the move? Instead, slow down and then turn, get your dog in position, draw a mental guideline from the judge to your dog, and start back. Begin to slow about three-quarters of the way back; you don't want to run over the judge or have to stop your dog suddenly, in which case it is certain to stop with legs askew. Walk your dog into a self-stand.

ment leg. Because most dogs will be somewhat erratic moving on the right, you need to switch back so that the dog is again on your left for the final leg heading back to the judge. In really big breeds switching sides is so difficult, and the judge can probably see enough of the dog on either side of the handler, that the side change is not essential, but in small breeds it is expected.

If you start off on any individual pattern, and your dog paces, plays, zigzags, jumps, or otherwise tries to destroy your chances, simply return to where you began and start again.

Some handlers who know they have a dog with absolutely horrible front and rear movement will try to hide it by running in a zigzag or by making the down and back into a sort of oval. Some judges will let them get away with it. The good judges will demand they do it right.

## The Final Inspection

As the last dog is moved you should have your dog set up and ready for the judge's final inspection. At this point most judges seem to play it by ear, so that it's often hard to be ready. They may do the following:

- They may have the dogs all pose side by side on the center mat so that fronts and rears can be compared.
- They may have two dogs at a time pose side by side on the examination table.
- They may ask each dog to move down and back again, or around

*"L": The first half of the "L" is like the first two legs of the "triangle." Then retrace your steps, but change hands so that the dog is on your right side, and so your body doesn't block the judge's view of the dog. When you get to the final leg heading directly back to the judge, place the dog back on your left side.*

the ring by itself, in pairs, or as a group.
- They may only move their favorites.
- They may move everybody, or they may even ignore their eventual first place winner because they have already decided upon it.

Never give up! I was in a large specialty class, and after the judge examined and moved all the dogs, she began to move only certain dogs—obviously her favorites. As dog after dog was moved, my disappointment grew; it was apparent we were not contenders. However, I decided that at least the spectators would see my dog at his best, so I never let down showing him. The judge ultimately moved every single dog in the class before coming to us. Then she finally told us to move— to first place! She later explained that first place was obvious to her; it was the other placements she had to work on.

*If you practice every possible scenario at home, you will be able to focus your attention on presenting your dog at its best in the ring. (Doberman pinscher)*

- They may place them tentatively and then rearrange them. At this point things tend to speed up and you must set your dog up quickly.

Because usually the judge is looking at profiles, set up the dog so that its profile looks good without worrying too much about straight fronts and rears. When you get a chance, or if the judge then starts to look at them, set them straight at that time. The exception, of course, is if the judge is clearly now first looking at fronts and rears, as when the dogs are set side by side. If your dog has a hideous rear, don't remind the judge of it by trying and trying to restack it. Constant attention to a fault, especially if you can't fix it, is like hanging a banner on your dog listing its bad points.

## Winning!

If you win, go to the first place marker and keep your dog looking good. Now is not the time to convince the judge that a horrible mistake was made, especially since you'll be going back to compete for Winners. Nor is it the time to convince the judge you have never won anything before by screaming hysterically in delight. The judge will need to record your armband number, so turn your arm so that both the judge and steward can see the number. The judge will then hand you the appropriate ribbon. Accept it with a gracious thank you whether it be blue, red, yellow, or white. If five dogs were competing in a class, and if yours was placed last, remember there is no fifth place ribbon so simply leave the ring.

If you won a trophy, the judge will also hand you a card. Take the card to the trophy table before BIS judging in order to claim your booty. Don't get your hopes up though—dog show trophies are notoriously useless! Nonetheless, be sure to write a short thank-you note to the donor.

# Climbing the Ladder

If there was more than one class, you will need to reenter the ring after the completion of the Open class. Dogs line up in the reverse order of their classes; that is, Open first, then American-Bred, and finally Puppy. Because the judge has already gone over all of the dogs, this class usually goes quickly, so be on your toes. If you win, again keep your dog looking good as you accept your ribbon, because you will be competing next for Best of Breed. In the more likely event that you lose, you will need to stay in the ring to compete for Reserve unless the dog that won Winners was the only one in its class.

## Reserve

Reserve is similar to First Runner-Up at a beauty pageant—if for any reason the winner cannot fulfill her duties (or if for any reason the winning dog is found ineligible for the win), the award (and points) would be awarded to the Reserve.

So the judge must determine which dog was the second best out of all entered. This means that if you placed second in any class, you need to stand by until after Winners just in case the dog that beat you wins the points. After Winners is chosen the dog that placed second to the Winners dog in its class must now enter the ring to compete for Reserve. The other class winners stay in the ring, quickly reposing their dogs, and the second-place dog usually takes the position of the dog that was just awarded Winners. This decision can be made in the blink of an eye, so act fast to get your dog posed. If you don't win Reserve, simply leave the ring.

## Things that Irritate Judges:
- being late for your class
- not following directions
- not paying attention
- feeding bait immediately before the judge examines the mouth
- throwing bait in the ring and not picking it up
- pointing out the good parts of your dog (by stroking and stretching those parts) as though the judge can't see them
- asking the judge hours later why your dog didn't win
- trying to influence a judge with comments about the dog's winning record
- being rough with a dog
- showing a dirty dog

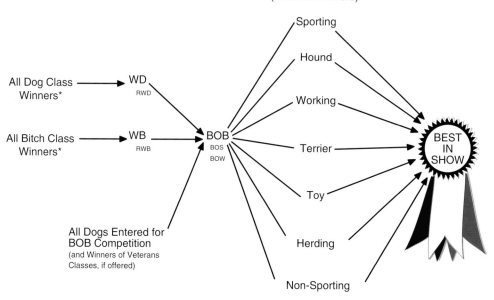

## AKC Competition

Group Competition
(All BOB Winners)

Sporting
Hound
Working
Terrier
Toy
Herding
Non-Sporting

All Dog Class Winners* → WD RWD

All Bitch Class Winners* → WB RWB

BOB BOS BOW

All Dogs Entered for BOB Competition
(and Winners of Veterans Classes, if offered)

BEST IN SHOW

**\*Dog and Bitch Classes**

| Puppy, 6–9 Months | | Bred by Exhibitor | |
|---|---|---|---|
| 1st | 3rd | 1st | 3rd |
| 2nd | 4th | 2nd | 4th |
| Puppy, 9–12 Months | | American Bred | |
| 1st | 3rd | 1st | 3rd |
| 2nd | 4th | 2nd | 4th |
| 12–18 Months | | Open | |
| 1st | 3rd | 1st | 3rd |
| 2nd | 4th | 2nd | 4th |
| Novice | | | |
| 1st | 3rd | | |
| 2nd | 4th | | |

**Ribbon Colors**

| | |
|---|---|
| BIS | Red, white, and blue |
| 1st Placements | Blue |
| 2nd | Red |
| 3rd | Yellow |
| 4th | White |
| BOB | Purple and gold |
| BOS | Red and white |
| BOW | Blue and white |
| WD and WB | Purple |
| RWD and RWB | Purple and white |

## Best of Breed

You probably won't have to worry about what comes next at your first show, but, for future reference, if you win Winners you will reenter the ring after Reserve Winners Bitch has been chosen. All of the champions entered for Best of Breed competition will enter the ring first, followed by the Winners Dog (WD), and then Winners Bitch (WB). Because the judge has already examined both Winners dogs, your dog will get a less intensive going over at this point. The Winners dog and bitch are often asked to gait around the ring together for direct comparison. In fact, after the last champion has been examined, both WD and WB should be posed so the judge can compare the two. The judge must make three decisions in this class:

1. Which is the best dog of that breed? This dog will be awarded Best of Breed (BOB).
2. Which is the best dog of the sex that is the opposite sex of the dog chosen Best of Breed? This is the Best of Opposite Sex (BOS) winner.
3. Which is the best nonchampion dog entered; that is, which is the better of the Winners Dog and Bitch? This dog is called Best of Winners (BOW).

Although the two Winners dogs are in contention for the BOB and BOS awards, they more often are defeated by the champions. But Best of Winners is extremely important because it influences the number of points won (see What's the Point?, page 92). These three winners line up in the order BOB, BOW, and BOS.

## The Group Ring

If the gods smile upon you and you somehow miraculously win Best of Breed, you can now be scared because you have received an invitation to the group ring, and this is where the big guns hang out, and also where people actually watch you. You don't have to attend, but you should. If a judge thinks enough

of your dog to give it a BOB, then you owe it to that judge to hang around and represent your breed in the group, especially if that same judge is judging the group.

Breeds enter the group ring lined up roughly by size and speed. But do not go first or second no matter how big or fast your dog is—not until you know what you're doing. Farther back in line just follow the lead of the handlers ahead of you and you will survive. Similarly, if you have a dog that must be posed on a table, be sure you get behind another breed that is shown on a table so that you can follow their lead. Pose your dog in the same place as the dog ahead of you as soon as that dog starts to gait. Everything is basically done the same as though you were showing in a very large class in a very large ring. Remember, though, that other judges often watch the groups, so even when relaxing don't let your dog look too hangdog. Tomorrow's judge may be watching!

*As the last dog is gaited back to the judge, the other competitors get back in line and pose their dogs in preparation for the judge's final inspection. The bulldog, traditionally the last dog in the non-sporting group, will have to pose quickly in order to be ready.*

*Toy group competition during the Westminster Kennel Club. It may feel like this many eyes are upon you in the ring, but at most shows very few people will be watching.*

Often, individuals in the group ring have lots of friends on the outside who will clap fanatically for their dog. Don't be upset because you can hear a pin drop when it's your dog's turn; it truly means nothing. Some astute judges demand that if a crowd can't cheer for every dog, they don't want to hear cheering at all.

Many group judges make a cut, keeping their group finalists in the ring and dismissing the remainder. Even top Best in Show dogs find themselves in the dismissed group, so just be aware that if you are in this group you are in good company, and remember—just getting to the group ring is a wonderful achievement. If you are left in as a finalist, go into your "two-minute offense" mode: Set up quickly, paying special attention to how the profile appears rather than perfecting fronts and rears. Keep your dog posed at all times. Once the cut is made, competition becomes intense. Don't be too disappointed if you don't get

one of the four placements available; "making the cut" gives you bragging rights as well. Congratulate the winners, and know that one day you will be one of them.

## Best in Show

If you win the group and are invited to Best in Show competition, you should leave the show to buy a lottery ticket. Unfortunately, you will have to wait until after Best in Show before you leave because this is a command performance—group winners *must* attend.

Best in Show competition is run the same way as group competition, except that there are only seven dogs in the ring. Don't let your dog relax as much as you might in any earlier competitions. Most judges do not make a cut, preferring to let the suspense build up until after they have marked their book. Then, ribbon in hand, in a hushed silence, they stand in the middle of the ring while seven handlers sweat and pray, and finally dramatically point to one supreme winner—the only dog that can leave the show that day undefeated.

If you win Best in Show you should quit while you are ahead and never enter another dog show!

## You Ought to Be in Pictures

You will probably want to have a picture made of an exciting win by the official dog show photographer. Ask the ring steward when the judge will be taking pictures, and stick around for the next session. Most people want a picture of anything from Winners on up, but a nice Reserve or first placement may be just as memorable. Several weeks later the photo or proof will arrive in the mail, and you will be expected to purchase it unless it's really a terrible picture.

Some people have pictures taken as an excuse to chat with the judge. Most judges have a busy schedule and have to squeeze photo sessions into it. They seldom have time to talk about your dog, and usually don't care to hear all about its illustrious show career. Certainly a remark that your dog just finished, or that its father was also BOB that day, is not out of place, but a recital of every win and every judge it's won under will not be appreciated.

Some exhibitors order an extra photo so they can send the judge a copy along with a short thank-you note for the win. Perhaps they reason that the judge will remember them the next time they show under them. Most judges are inundated with such photos, and unless it was a particularly important win, probably won't be terribly thrilled to get more. Still, if it was a thrilling win for you, that's sufficient cause. Do not be tempted to send the judge a thank-you gift; that's called a bribe.

Simply because you won under a judge doesn't mean that judge loves your dog and will always place it first. Too many exhibitors have traveled hundreds of miles for

The pinnacle: Best in Show at Westminster! The Westminster Kennel Club Show is open only to dogs that are already Champions, and is the most prestigious show in the United States. Note that the BIS ribbon at Westminster is traditionally purple and gold, rather than red, white, and blue, as it is at other shows. (Clumber spaniel)

a "sure thing" under a judge who had previously given their dog a big win, only to place last. Different competition and different circumstances will always play a part. Keep in mind as well, that most judges do not like to be followed from show to show by exhibitors!

## The Worst that Could Happen

The worst thing that could happen during a show would be if your dog attacked a person or another dog, or was in turn attacked. Such scenarios are uncommon, but if you have any doubts about your own dog's ability to be well-behaved in public, keep it home. Otherwise,

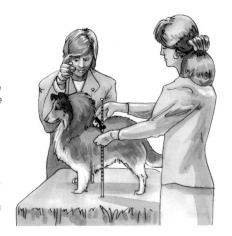

*In breeds for which height is a possible disqualification, the judge may ask to measure any or all of the entries in a class. The dog is posed normally, and the measuring wicket is passed over its rear until the wicket reaches the withers, where the height is measured.*

there are several ways to lose that seem pretty awful at the time, but some are not really that bad. Remember, it's one judge's opinion on one day. Many dogs that have had ribbons withheld for lack of merit have gone on to become group winners at other shows.

**Excusal:** Dogs can be excused from judging for a number of reasons, the most common being that the dog is lame. Some judges won't excuse a dog unless it's on three legs, and others will excuse at the slightest hint of the dog favoring a foot. Dogs can also be excused because they appear ill, or because they will not allow the judge to examine them. Excusal is not a mark of shame; some handlers will even ask that their dog be excused rather than have it continue to compete when it is not at its best. It is often kinder for a shy dog to be excused than for a judge to force an examination on it, which may only result in further frightening it and possibly put the judge at risk for getting bitten.

If there is a suspicion that the height or weight of a dog may be a disqualification, the dog will be excused if the judge is unable to measure or weigh the dog.

Dogs can also be excused for having foreign substance on their coat or body. Excessive powder or chalk, hair spray, hair dye, nose dye, or painted toenails would all be cause for excusal.

Finally, dogs can be excused for menacing behavior toward a person and for acting in a manner that would suggest the judge could not approach it safely.

A dog that has been excused is not counted as having been in competition for the purpose of computing points.

**Withholding:** In some entries the quality may be so poor that the judge feels no dog is deserving of winning points, a blue ribbon, or any ribbon at all. Under these circumstances, the judge has the option of withholding an award. In a class of two dogs, for example, the judge may only award a red (second place) and yellow (third place) ribbon, or the judge may withhold all ribbons. He or she may award first placements, but then choose to withhold the Winners award, so that no points are won.

Dogs from whom all ribbons are withheld are not counted as being in competition for the purpose of computing points.

**Disqualification:** In all breeds male dogs must have two normal testicles normally descended in the scrotum, or they will be disqualified. Many breed standards contain specific disqualifications, in which the presence or lack of a particular trait is so vital to the breed, that without it the dog cannot be allowed to compete. Most common are disqualifications based upon height, which is measured at the withers, or highest point of the shoulder blade, with the dog in a normal show stance. A dog disqualified under these provisions by three different judges may not be shown again.

Dogs that attack people, blind or deaf dogs, castrated or spayed dogs (except in certain classes), or dogs that have been surgically altered in any way but those commonly allowed (allowed changes would be removal of dewclaws, or cropped ears or tail) can also be disqualified. A dog disqualified once under these provisions has all awards at that show canceled and may not be shown again.

The following procedures would render a dog subject to disqualification:

- Correction of entropion, ectropion, trichiasis, or distichiasis (all eyelid anomalies)
- Trimming, removal, or tattooing of the third eyelid (nictitating membrane)
- Insertion of an artificial eye
- Correction of harelip, cleft palate, stenotic nares (pinched nostrils), or resection of an elongated palate
- Any procedure (other than that permitted by individual breed standards) to change ear set or carriage

- The use of bands or braces on the teeth, restorative dental procedures, or any alteration of the dental arcade
- The removal of excess skin folds, or of skin patches that would alter markings
- Correction of inguinal, scrotal, or perineal hernias
- Alteration of the location of the testes or the insertion of an artificial testicle
- Surgery for hip dysplasia, osteochondritis desicans (OCD), patellar luxation, or femoral head resection (all orthopedic problems with hereditary bases)
- Alteration of the set or carriage of the tail

A disqualification is serious, and you should consult the AKC representative at that show to find out what, if any, recourse you have. In some cases you can apply to the AKC to have the dog reinstated.

**Suspension:** A person who has been suspended is really in the doghouse. During a period of suspension, you cannot sell, breed, or show a dog. This applies to dogs you own or co-own. You can attend an AKC event as a spectator only. You are in AKC limbo.

Suspension can result from any number of activities determined to be detrimental to the sport of purebred dogs, including:

- a conviction of cruelty to animals
- putting false information on registration materials
- showing a dog that has been surgically altered

- substitution of dogs
- unsportsmanlike conduct at an AKC event, such as yelling at the judge, refusing to accept a ribbon, throwing a ribbon to the ground, loudly voicing dissatisfaction with judging, using obscene language, and fighting
- failure to follow stated rules
- arguing with parking officials
- damaging motel rooms during a dog event

Suspensions may be accompanied by a fine.

**Awards disallowed:** If a dog is shown in a class for which it is ineligible, and wins a ribbon or even points, the discrepancy will be discovered by the AKC when the win is officially recorded. The AKC will send a letter asking that the ribbons be returned and informing the owner that the awards are disallowed. If points were involved, the reserve winner will be awarded the points. Failure to return ribbons or trophies can be grounds for suspension; therefore, you should keep all ribbons you win for a few months after a show. The most common reason that an award would be disallowed would be for showing a puppy in the wrong age division, or a novice dog that had more than three first places, or a Bred by Exhibitor dog not owned by the breeder or family. The AKC has a tendency to disallow without asking any questions, so if you feel they have done so unfairly you can ask to discuss the matter or write a letter of protest.

# The After Show

If you are among the 99.9 percent of the competitors who do not win Best of Breed, you should still stay at the show until the bitter end. Take the chance to socialize your dog. Treat it like a winner whether or not the ribbons reflected its true worth. Visit the booths and buy it a pig ear or other delicacy that will leave a good taste in its mouth about dog shows. Watch the other breeds, and study the different handling techniques. Meander around the grooming sections and spy on everybody's "secret" grooming techniques, most of which would be gladly divulged to you if you only ask. Dog shows are populated by people itching to tell other people how to do everything. If you can take criticism, ask someone in your breed or a related breed to critique your dog or handling.

It is tempting to try to pattern your own handling after the handlers in the Best in Show ring, and this is in part a good idea—but always try to find out why. What works for the handler with the Irish setter will look awfully foolish with your Boston terrier, and some good handlers have bad habits that they win in spite of, not because of. Still, assume that even their worst habits are going to be infinitely better than your best at the moment, and try to pick out styles and techniques with which you feel comfortable.

The best handlers know that every dog is different, and they adapt their handling technique to the individual dog. The turning point in my most successful dog's career came from a loss. We were competing against a favorite of mine, a dog known for his flashy showmanship. As he baited and danced, I tried in vain to get my dog to even look at the bait. The judge studied the two of them, and of course chose the other dog. The judge had seen a master at his trade versus a rank amateur when it came to baiting. I realized that as long as we tried to beat such masters at their own game, we would continue to look second rate, and we would lose. Instead, I thought about what my dog was good at: standing like a statue at the end of the lead and looking snobbishly down her nose at everyone. She won the group the first time we tried it, and she was almost never defeated after that. Judge after judge commented on her arrogant attitude. If you can't join 'em, beat 'em!

A final word of warning about post-showtime. Your friends will tell you that you should have won. Thank them for being such good friends; sometimes they will even be right. Sometimes other people in the breed will get together for a gripe fest about the judging. Don't get too carried away; you may not agree with the judging, but judging is subjective and it would be impossible for everyone to agree. Gripe a little if it makes you feel better, but don't let it take over your day. Your friends may also want to tell you every little thing you did wrong.

Don't let it upset you; this is harder than it looks!

Whenever beginning a new sport it can be discouraging to not be the best right away. Dog shows are one of the very few sports in which the first-time amateur is pitted against lifelong professionals. Yes, the professionals will be more skilled than you. They had better be. That makes it all the more fun to beat them! A good judge can see a good dog, and dogs, not handlers, are what dog shows are all about.

## Do Unto Others

Dog showing is a civilized sport, and as such, one performed with considerable restraint when it comes to dirty tricks. Don't accidentally or purposefully try to win by messing up your competition. Your competitors may give you the benefit of the doubt at first, and give you a polite warning, but beware: they know a lot more dirty tricks than you do and if you keep it up, they may band together and make you the target of the all of their tricks combined.

Whether accidental, or on purpose, be careful not to be the victim or the perpetrator of the following:
- Stepping on a dog's paw
- Spilling a drink on a dog's coat
- Frightening a dog
- Distracting a male dog with a bitch in season
- Running up too close behind the dog in front when moving

*The handler stands out of the judge's way while ensuring that his dog is steady and content. (Wirehaired dachshund)*

- Slamming on brakes unpredictably so the person behind you will give the appearance (to the judge) that they were running up on your dog
- Setting up too close to the dog in front when standing, so that the dog behind is breathing down the other's back, or the handler behind keeps brushing against the dog in front
- Backing your dog into the dog set up behind
- Making a lot of noise when behind a skittish dog
- Intimidating another handler
- Doing anything that could endanger the well-being of another dog or person

If any of the above things happen to you, you can either remove yourself from the situation, ask the other party to stop, or report the situation to the AKC rep.

# Problem-Solving

### What to do if:

- your dog is not entered in the class you had meant for it to be in: See the superintendent. Your entry form will be with them, and if *they* made a mistake, they will correct it. If *you* made a mistake, too bad. With the exception of entering in the wrong sex or age division, most mistakes cannot be corrected.
- you lose your armband: Just rustle up another with the same number, or find a discarded one, turn it inside out, and write your number on it by hand.
- your dog goes lame: Examine the paw for foreign objects. Massage the leg. Trot the dog to see if you can work it out. Don't try to show a lame dog. Inform the steward that your dog will be absent.
- your dog begins to limp in the ring: Ask to go last while you try to work it out. If the judge has to excuse the dog for lameness, it is not a bad reflection on the dog.
- your dog defecates in the aisles of the show: Ask the nearest ring steward to call for cleanup, locate the cleanup crew yourself, or clean it up yourself.
- your dog starts to defecate or urinate in the ring: Just stop; it happens. Dragging a dog around will only distribute the mess and make you look bad. If the judge or ring steward didn't see the deed you will need to discreetly ask the steward to call for

cleanup. Then you'll want to step away from it so the judge won't know whose dog did it!

- your dog acts like it might bite the judge: Ask to be excused, for the sake of the judge, the dog, and you.

- your dog refuses to budge in the ring: Try coaxing it forward with bait. If it is a small dog, carry it a few steps and then put it down. Pull it for a few steps with the lead, but don't drag it around the entire ring. If your dog won't walk, you're not going to win anyway, so don't make yourself look bad by dragging the dog like a pull toy, as well as making the experience for the dog that much worse.

- you feel sick or faint in the ring: Inform the steward. If need be, hand the steward your dog and leave the ring. Somebody will almost certainly be happy to finish showing it for you.

- you fall in the ring: Make sure your dog isn't too frightened or tries to run away. If it gets loose and others try to catch it, inform them if this is not a good idea. Take your time getting up; if you are up to it, finish showing, but if not, ask the steward if you can be excused or if you can have another handler take over.

- the person who was supposed to show your dog couldn't make it in time, and you've had to take the dog in yourself: Get as far back in line as possible. If the preferred handler shows up before your dog is examined individually by

the judge, that person can ask the ring steward to ask the judge for a change of handler. The request is usually granted.

- you are late for your class: Ask the steward if you are too late to be allowed in. If you are, don't let it ruin your life. It happens to everybody eventually.

- you miss your class entirely: Sometimes, only if you were the only entrant in your class, a very nice judge will let you go in after another class as long as Winners has not yet been chosen.

- your dog acts up in the ring: Whatever you do, don't lose your temper or be rough with your dog. It will make you look like a novice, bad owner, and poor sport, and will be terrible training for your dog. Besides, rough handling is against AKC rules and can result in suspension.

- the dog starts fidgeting, or you can't seem to stack it properly:

*Don't let your dog get hidden in a corner, as is the second dog in line. (Note the typical and distinctive pose of the German shepherd dog, with the right rear leg placed in an extreme forward position.)*

Walk it in a small clockwise circle and start over. Give it a little break if time permits.

- you lose: Act like you won. Smile and pet your dog as you leave the ring. It will baffle onlookers, make you look like a confident exhibitor and good sport, and most of all, be good training for your dog. Be sure to congratulate the winners.
- you think the judge is a moron: Don't show under that judge again. If you believe an AKC rule was violated, ask at the superintendent's desk to speak to the AKC representative and explain the situation.
- you win: Take it with the same graciousness as you would a loss. Remember, when you win, there is someone else who is very disappointed because they lost. Being a good sport means being both a good loser and a good winner.

## What's the Point?

As you clutch that wonderful purple Winners ribbon in your trembling hand you will eventually ask: "How many points?" The answer is usually straightforward, but there are several situations that at first seem to require some sort of new math.

### The Basics

The requirements for an AKC championship are that your dog win 15 points under at least three different judges. Included in these 15 points must be two majors, which are wins of three, four, or five points, won under two different judges. The number of points depends upon the number of dogs defeated, and will vary with breed, sex, and geographical location. The United States is divided into regions. The AKC computes the number of dogs in each breed competing in the last year and adjusts the point schedule so that a certain percentage of shows are projected to yield one, two, three, four, or five points, with the majors being by far the scarcest. The point schedule is updated every May, and the current schedule for that region is printed in every show catalog.

Take for example the 1995 Division 4 point schedule for Brittanys, as shown at the top of page 93.

Let's say you have a Brittany bitch. The number competing is 7–7–1–3. If you win:

- **Winners Bitch (WB):** If your bitch wins Winners, and seven bitches were in competition, then the win is worth two points.
- **Best of Winners (BOW):** If your bitch wins Winners for two points, and then wins Best of Winners, you will win points equal to what the Winners Dog (WD) won. The dog won't lose its points, and these points won't be added to your original two. In other words, if there were seven dogs (males) in competition, your Best of Winners bitch would win three points in place of two.

If your bitch goes Best of Winners over a WD who goes Best of Opposite Sex over Specials, it is

| Points | | 1 | | 2 | | 3 | | 4 | | 5 | |
|---|---|---|---|---|---|---|---|---|---|---|---|
| Sex | | D | B | D | B | D | B | D | B | D | B |
| # competing | | 2 | 2 | 4 | 5 | 7 | 8 | 8 | 10 | 10 | 13 |

important to figure the points that the male will get for BOS before figuring the BOW points. In our example, the win would be worth four points.

- **Best of Opposite Sex over Specials:** If your bitch wins Winners for two points, and then is awarded Best of Opposite Sex over the champion bitches, add the number of bitches competing in BOB competition to the number of class bitches. If there were seven class bitches and three champion bitches, this totals ten bitches and is worth four points instead of your two original points.
- **Best of Breed over Specials:** If your bitch wins Best of Breed, count all of the class bitches, and add to that number all dogs and bitches competing in BOB. In our example, if there were seven class bitches, three champion bitches, and one champion dog, then this totals eleven and is worth four points. Note that had the WD gone BOB, defeating the same eleven dogs would have given it a five-point major.

Remember, do not count absent, excused, disqualified, or moved up dogs, or any dogs that have had all awards withheld. Do not count dogs competing in any non-regular classes. You do not add points together on a given day; you only substitute a higher point count for a lower one.

You can also win points by winning Group First or Best in Show. If you win Group First, you would win the highest number of points that any dog in that group had won. If your border terrier won two points by winning BOB, and then won the group, and a Lakeland terrier had won three points, then your dog would win three, instead of two, points. If you win Best in Show, you would win the highest number of points that any dog in the show won. So if your border terrier then won Best in Show, and a whippet had won a five-point major, your dog would receive five, instead of three, points.

When confused about the number of dogs defeated, check the judge's sheets located next to the superintendent's table. These are copies of the official judge's book that the judge marks in the ring, and are usually available within an hour after the breed is judged. If you are still confused, ask the superintendent. Don't ever leave the show with a lingering question about points. You can call the AKC show records department at a later date to check, but it's much easier to get it settled before heading home.

## Points of Contention

If you want to quickly become the most unpopular person in your breed, then enter shows and don't show up when the entry is just barely a major. Your fellow exhibitors may have traveled hundreds of miles for the chance to compete for a major, and when the major doesn't materialize, you had better not only be in the hospital, but in intensive care, to dodge their wrath. Always carefully examine the entries and number of points available when the judging schedule arrives. If it is exactly a major, get to the show or get to the hospital.

There are those exhibitors who actually are present at the show and pull their entry for the express purpose of breaking the major. Driven by spite, they assume a certain dog will win so these exhibitors break the major in order to prevent that doggy from finishing. This is surely one of the dumbest things that anyone can do, because half the time the dog they assumed would win doesn't. And if a competitor's dog is so good that it keeps beating yours, your best bet is to help it finish as fast as possible and get it out of your way.

What if you are the unlucky one who is the victim of a broken major? If your dog only needs majors to finish its championship, then some people consider it less than sporting to show your dog and possibly win the single points that another dog might desperately need. In general, if there is any chance at all that you could win a major, either by going BOW or BOB over Specials, show your dog. In fact, no one would blame you if you showed your dog no matter when the major broke. After all, you've made the effort to get to the show so you might as well show.

If you are lucky enough to finish your dog before the last day of a show weekend, you may find yourself in a good sportsmanship quagmire. You can move your dog up to BOB competition by filing the appropriate forms at the superintendent's desk by one half hour before the next day's show begins, but in so doing you may end up breaking the major for the remaining dogs. If you have a good chance of winning BOB, then you should probably go ahead and move up. After all, the major will still be available to the other dogs if they go BOB over your dog. If there's little chance of going BOB regardless, then ask your fellow competitors if they would prefer that you move your dog up or keep it in the classes. Usually they will prefer the latter. Sometimes your competitors will ask that you keep your dog in the classes and show it poorly, so that their dog can win. Don't.

# Chapter Eight
# Problem Dogs

Every dog is a potential problem dog, because no dog is perfect. Each dog has its personal shortcomings that must be minimized, as well as its own idiosyncratic behaviors. The job of the handler is to minimize the dog's shortcomings and to help it to show itself to its best advantage.

## Gaiting Problems

**Crabbing:** Crabbing, or running sideways, most often results from a dog that steps too far forward with its rear legs, so that the dog must run at an angle in order to avoid stepping on its front feet with its rear. Shortening the stride by moving at a slower pace will help, but dogs can also crab out of habit. Practice gaiting your crabber next to a wall or curb. Gaiting with the dog on your right side can also help alleviate the problem. Practice only with your dog on the right, and then switch to the left side only in the show ring. If the dog is crabbing with its front toward you, it could be because it is twisting around in an attempt to get your bait. Try showing without bait.

**Pacing:** Dogs are judged at a trot, a gait wherein diagonal legs move together. In pacing, the two legs on the same side of the body move in unison. In many long-legged breeds, if the dog gradually speeds up from a walk, it will at some point approach a pace. Most will break into a trot, but some will continue to simply speed up and end up in a pace. Judges hate pacing dogs, and next to biting the judge, having your dog pace is about the surest way to lose. Still, a surprising number of exhibitors cannot tell when their dogs are pacing. Look for these clues:

*The pacing dog (top) moves both legs on the same side in unison. The trotting dog (bottom) moves diagonal legs in unison.*

**95**

- The legs on the same side of the body are moving back and forth in unison. If the dog is on your left, watch its two right legs to see if they move as though hobbled together.
- The dog sways from side to side.

The simplest way to avoid pacing is to avoid easing into a trot. Start out with a burst of speed, even if you then must slow down to get to your dog's best speed. If this doesn't work, hold the dog's head up with your hand under its chin for the first few steps. If the dog is pacing and you're already moving, give the lead a sharp tug to the right, ideally when the right legs are both off the ground. This will often pull the dog off balance enough so that it must change into the more balanced trotting gait. If nothing works, turn around and start over.

Watch your dog when it gaits. Few things look sillier than a handler confidently striding around the ring, oblivious to their dog pacing alongside.

**Tale of the tail:** Proper tail carriage is a function of both conformation and temperament, and varies from breed to breed. In breeds in which the tail should be carried high over the back, it is vital to have a happy, confident dog. Placing the tail over the back before moving will help in many breeds (such as Pekingese), while in some others (Afghan hounds, for example) scratching beneath the base of the tail before gaiting will encourage the dog to hold it up while moving. In most breeds it is per-

fectly acceptable to hold the tail in proper position while the dog is stacked. If the dog will hold the tail correctly on its own, so much the better, but judges do not usually expect them to do so unaided.

Breeds in which tail carriage can be too high can also present a problem. Tails carried over the back, or "gay" tails, can totally ruin the outline of these dogs. To make matters worse, the happier the dog gets, the higher the tail goes. Yet you don't want to dampen the dog's spirits. Some people try to tap the tail when it comes up, but it can be hard to discourage a gay tail without also discouraging a happy dog. Most people just try to keep such dogs a little less excited, realizing that a tail carried too high is a small price to pay for a happy show dog.

There are those unscrupulous individuals who will "fix" tails that don't behave properly. Tails that have had the ligament cut to cure a gay tail are easily spotted, because they hang like a limp rope, and are never raised at all. The tail is an important balance tool in many breeds; not only is surgical alteration of it against AKC rules, ethical considerations, and all ideas of sportsmanship, but it also is detrimental to the dog.

# Behavior Problems

### Hang-Dog Head Carriage

Most breeds look their best when they strut around the ring with the head held high. With increasing speed, however, it is natural for the head to be extended forward when trotting, and most judges will find this perfectly acceptable. It is the dog that decides to never carry its head up that presents a problem.

Shy and scared dogs may slink along with their heads down. The cure is to work on their confidence. Happy and confident dogs tend to carry their heads up, so your number one task is to work on making showing fun. The head will come up in time.

**The lead:** In many breeds it is customary to show dogs on tight leads. Usually a non-choking fairly wide lead is used, and it is often held so tightly that the front legs don't put all of their weight on the ground. This is seen in many terriers and in cocker spaniels. In most toy breeds, a fine non-choke lead is used that is kept taught. In large powerful breeds, again a tight lead is generally used in order to keep the dog under control. But in many breeds, judges prefer to see the dogs on a loose lead, and in some dogs trying to hold the dog's head up will only result in choking it.

Experiment with different types of lead. A metal choke chain may actually make your dog show in a livelier fashion. Twirling the collar around so that the lead comes off under the dog's neck will very often cause the dog to carry its head high. Pull the lead forward, not up, and the dog will often respond by throwing its head back. For dogs that are sensitive about leads touching their ears, try letting the collar fall down around their withers.

**The ring vacuum:** Some small dogs discover that the ring mats are littered with dropped bait, and consider it their duty to sniff out every crumb and vacuum them up. Never let your dog eat bait off the ground. Reward it instead with bait from your hand every time it looks up. Some handlers try rubbing something like Vick's VapoRub on the dog's nose in an attempt to interfere with its ability to smell, but this should be tried only as a last resort.

Remember that different breeds have naturally different head carriages. A bloodhound that wants to sniff the ground shouldn't be faulted for this natural tendency, and some breeds (such as the borzoi) are built in such a way that extremely high head carriage is not natural. Still, the style is for a head held high, so you may have to work by rewarding your dog with a piece of bait for holding up its head.

### Shyness

Many breeds of dogs, particularly some of the toys, sighthounds, and herding breeds, can be overwhelmed upon finding themselves surrounded by thousands of people and dogs. Dogs that bait and pose and act like stallions in the backyard may suddenly turn into wilting touch-me-nots. Early socialization in the form of puppy kindergarten classes and handling classes are the best means of prevention for shyness, but sometimes no matter what you do, you will have to cope with a shy dog.

Building a dog's confidence is not an easy task, and there are no quick cures. The key word is *patience*. You do not build a dog's confidence by losing your temper, by scolding it, or by thrusting it into situations that terrify it; nor do you build confidence by coddling it. You must walk a fine line in which you will challenge your dog to be brave, but never overwhelm it.

People with shy dogs tend to react in one of several wrong ways. Some hug the dog to them, petting and consoling it. Such action only serves to convince the dog that its fear is reasonable, and reinforces its fearful behavior.

Other owners become disgusted at their dogs, and jerk them around until they behave. When the dog shies away, they punish it and force it to stand. This obviously will only cause the dog to dread the situation even more.

The most common wrong response is to decide to train the dog by subjecting it to the most overwhelming situations possible, with the expectation that the dog will get used to it and won't be scared at all when confronted with a slightly less scary situation. A similar approach, called "flooding," was popular in psychotherapy many years ago. It didn't work with people, and it doesn't work with dogs.

You want to teach your dog to be brave, and you don't do that by scaring it. You do it by exposing the dog to ever so slightly more intimidating situations, none so intimidating that it cannot eventually feel at ease. In this way you are teaching the dog to relax in strange situations. If you take it too far, you will accomplish nothing but to teach the dog to be afraid.

Shy dogs may suffer from a fear of unfamiliar dogs, unfamiliar humans, or unfamiliar situations. Dogs that are afraid of certain situations usually do not know what is expected of them in those situations. This is easily remedied by teaching the dog a few simple obedience commands. Teach the dog sit/stay or stand/stay in the security of your home. Then practice in your yard, your neighborhood, and eventually, obedience or handling classes. Don't teach the exercise at the class; class is only a place to practice. Now when your dog doesn't know how to cope with a situation, you will tell it how. By sitting on command, the dog at least knows that it is doing the right thing. In addition, you can then praise your dog for its actions, and reward it with a tidbit for its good behavior.

**Fear of people:** Dogs that are afraid of strange people are more afraid of the attention of these people than the people themselves. Like shy humans, they can handle being in a room full of strangers until they become the center of attention. One of the worst pieces of advice commonly given to dog owners is to take their shy dogs to a place full of people and have the people pet the dog and go over it as a judge would. Eventually that may be possible, but at first you are better off asking strangers to totally ignore your dog. Let any advances be on the dog's part. Eventually the dog may sneak up behind and sniff them, at which time the person should still ignore the dog. The stranger should offer the dog a tasty treat without looking at the dog, then offer the treat while looking at the dog, then touch the dog and offer the treat, until the dog allows itself to be examined. The key is to take everything extremely slowly, and never push the dog too hard.

*Propping up a shy dog only encourages it to lean on its handler. When the handler kneels in front of the shy dog, it cannot lean on the handler so easily.*

**Sedatives:** Some exhibitors may be tempted to use sedatives as a shortcut. The use of sedatives in a dog being shown is against AKC rules and grounds for suspension. Drugged dogs can be spotted by their sometimes overly calm demeanor accompanied by dilated pupils. The most commonly used drug is acepromazine, which has the further drawback that it can result in incoordination and has been implicated in deaths of animals while drugged in transit.

Dog behavior therapists will sometimes prescribe diazapam (valium) as a training tool only. If a dog is so shy that it cannot calm down in even the mildest of situations, an antianxiety medication can help facilitate learning. Acepromazine is ineffective as a learning drug because it is technically a dissociative agent, meaning that it

enables the dog to dissociate itself from its surroundings; thus, the dog doesn't remember the so-called learning experience. Again, the use of valium in competition is not only unethical and illegal, but probably counterproductive as your dog would very likely not be moving or showing at its best. The use of drugs—for training only—should be undertaken only under direction of a veterinarian.

**In the ring:** Some dogs may never totally overcome their shyness. The degree to which a judge will fault such a dog will depend upon the judge and the breed of dog. Shyness is more readily forgiven in a saluki than it is in a German shepherd dog. When showing a dog that is shy of other dogs, try to be last in line so that another dog is not on your dog's heels, otherwise, remind the handler behind you to be especially careful not to run up on your dog. Enter a large class so that your dog has time to settle down before the judge goes over it. If possible, stand or kneel in front of your dog when the judge approaches it. It is tempting to stand next to your dog with one hand ready to prop its rear up, but shy dogs will lean into you and you will end up almost holding your dog. If you are in front of your dog, it cannot lean into you, but it will still be able to look at you and gain confidence. Outdoor shows are usually better for shy dogs.

*The most well constructed dog will never win unless it can show itself off.*

Finally, one must always question the advisability of showing a shy dog at all. If the experience is to be that painful for the animal, perhaps it is best allowed to stay home. If your dog is so fearful that there is the slightest chance of it snapping at the judge, do not show it. When it comes to breeding, remember that shyness has a hereditary component and may very likely manifest itself in any offspring.

### Aggression

Less commonly, dogs have a problem with aggression. Dogs may snap out of fear or out of aggressive tendencies. In almost every such case, the dog should *not* be shown. Period. If you absolutely *must* show, ask the opinion of a very experienced dog behaviorist. Then ask a very experienced professional handler to show your dog for you. Warn the professional of your concerns. A dog that could harm a person or another dog has no place at a dog show. Too many people bring dogs to shows that they cannot physically control, and too often, other people and dogs pay a dear price.

### Dullness

The most common problem that beginners have with their dogs is dullness. As the other dogs bait and pose with every muscle tensed, the dull dog stands like a sack of potatoes. The other dogs stride around the ring, heads up and tails flagging; the dull dog drags and shuffles its feet, head and tail hanging.

It may have the best conformation in the ring, but who can see it?

Dull dogs are hard to cure. Newcomers end up with them because they too often emphasize rigid obedience training and they overtrain for shows. Most new owners think show training consists of teaching the dog to stand still and trot, but they forget to train attitude. When they get to the show, they too often take out their own nervousness on the dog and the dog's initial show experiences are seldom happy ones. To add to the problem, the dog is often tired from being dragged all around the show before it enters the ring.

You can try to retrain a dull dog. Start by baiting. Teach the dog to catch bait, and make a big game out of it. Set up a practice ring at home, or if you attend a training class, ask to be allowed to just bait and play with your dog. Be unpredictable. Quit early. Teach your dog that the ring is where fun happens, and keep it wanting more.

When at the show, don't walk the dog all around the show. Let it rest in its cage before showtime. Don't feed your dog a big breakfast the day of the show; stuffed dogs are sleepy dogs, and far less likely to bait. If possible, have a friend get the dog ready and walk it ringside. Then, show up at the last moment so that the dog is still happily greeting you as you whisk it into the ring. Let your dog bait and play while the other dogs are being examined. Use a chain choke collar. As a last resort, have a stranger show your dog. Dogs are more attentive to handlers they don't know.

## Overexcitability

If your dog is overexcited at shows, you have the easiest problem to solve of all; the cure is age and experience. You hope your new puppy is overly excited, because if it acts like a seasoned show dog its first time out, it will probably end up as a dull dog in adulthood. If you must calm your dog, walk or even jog it a while before showing it. Don't bring bait into the ring if it makes your dog too crazy. Use a chain choke and keep it high on the neck. Try to be first in line so that your dog doesn't try to chase the dog in front of it. Speak in a soft, soothing, but firm voice. Attend obedience classes and teach your dog some simple commands.

The worst excuse a handler can have is that the dog wouldn't show or behave. The handler's job is to shape the dog's behavior so that it looks as good—even better—in the ring as it does in the yard. If your dog can't do that, blame yourself, not the dog.

## Chapter Nine

# Other Fields to Conquer

The world of dogs has such a variety of activities that your dog would be exhausted if you tried to participate in everything. One advantage that the exhibitor with only one or two dogs has is the ability to dabble in several different areas of competition. A dog that can boast titles in conformation, obedience, agility, and field trial competitions is a superb example of its breed and what it has to offer, as well as a testimony to the dedication of its owner.

*England is home to the prestigious Cruft's Dog Show, which attracted some 20,000 entries in 1996. (Whippet)*

CRUFTS
BEST IN SHOW

## Showing Abroad

Dog shows are held all over the world, and if you like to travel, you can acquire titles in any country in which quarantines allow your dog to enter. In fact, some travel agencies specialize in dog show excursions all over the world. Each country has its own requirements for championships, and may have slightly different standards for the breeds. The largest international organization, the Fédération Cynologique Internationale (FCI), awards the prestigious International Championship, and once a year sponsors the huge World Dog Show in a different country. Four certificates of quality must be earned under four different judges, one of whom must be from a continent other than the one where the show is held. Some breeds must pass a working test before being awarded a championship, and all certificates must be earned after the dog is 15 months of age.

Mexico has similar requirements, except that only two of the four certificates must be earned after the age of 15 months. Some breeds must also have OFA certificates or working titles. Shows in Mexico are held under the auspices of the Federación Canofila Mexicana.

Canada is the country most often invaded by exhibitors from south of the border. Shows are similar to AKC shows, but are usually much smaller and more relaxed. Some breeds are categorized differently than with the AKC (most notably dachshunds, the three "Belgian" breeds, Chihuahuas, English toy spaniels, and shih tzu). Classes are Junior Puppy, Senior Puppy, Canadian-bred, Bred by Exhibitor, and Open. Class procedure is similar, with the only difference being that after BOB is chosen, all the Puppy Class winners compete for BOB Puppy. The adult BOB winner must compete in the group, or all awards won that day will be forfeited. After each group, the BOB puppies compete for best puppy in group, and after BIS, BIS puppy competition is held.

To become a Canadian champion, a dog must win ten points under three different judges. The point system is the same for all breeds: one point for two dogs competing, two points for three to five dogs, three points for six to nine dogs, four points for ten to twelve dogs, and five points for thirteen or more in competition.

Even in the United States, there are dog shows sanctioned by non-AKC organizations such as the United Kennel Club, States Kennel Club, World Wide Kennel Club, American Rare Breed Association,

*The World Show attracts entrants from all over the world. (Alaskan malamute and Afghan hound)*

and some other small kennel clubs. These events are usually less formal, and much smaller, than AKC shows, but are still fun.

The United Kennel Club (UKC) is the second largest registry in the United States. UKC shows can be entered the morning of the show; there are no superintendents, and neither professional handlers nor baiting are allowed in the rings. All of the information needed to enter a show can be found in the UKC official publication, *Bloodlines* (see Useful Addresses and Literature, page 139). To become a UKC champion, a dog must win 100 points. Classes for non-champions are divided by age and sex, and the winner of each class receives five points, regardless of the number of dogs in that class. Best of its sex wins additional points, and Best of Breed even more. Champions compete against each other for the title of Grand Champion.

# Child's Play

**Junior showmanship** classes are offered at all AKC all-breed shows, and are open to youngsters from 10 to 18 years of age. Their purpose is to promote good sportsmanship, handling ability, and a lifelong interest and responsible attitude toward purebred dogs and dog shows. Juniors are judged on their presentation of the dog, which includes proper grooming of both the dog and themselves, handling, and demeanor. Although the dog is not judged, a well-trained dog is an asset. The dog must be owned by the Junior or someone in the family or household. Sometimes breeders will make finished champions available to sincere Juniors on co-ownership as a means of helping out a newcomer and, through them, the future of the sport.

Contact the AKC for a copy of the complete Rules and Regulations for Junior Showmanship. Classes are divided by age (Junior: at least

*Junior showmanship can help build self-esteem in youngsters, and for some, the beginning of a successful career as a professional handler. (English setter)*

10 but under 14 years, and Senior: at least 14 but under 18 years on the day of the show) and by experience (Novice: having won fewer than three first placements, and Open: having won at least three first placements in Novice with competition). Regional and national competitions are held, and the best Juniors can handle better than 99 percent of the adult exhibitors at a show. In fact, much can be learned by watching the Open Junior Showmanship classes at a large show.

# Mind Games

**Obedience trials** allow dogs and owners to demonstrate their ability to work as a team. Some people feel that obedience is populated by dogs that couldn't make it as show dogs, but even Westminster Best in Show dogs have sported obedience titles. And obedience aficionados might be tempted to assert that conformation rings are full of dogs that couldn't succeed in obedience!

Some breeds have a natural aptitude for obedience. Poodles, golden retrievers, border collies, Shetland sheepdogs, and some other breeds that were bred for duties requiring human direction seem to excel. But don't despair if your dog is not one of the "gifted" breeds. Any breed can get at least the Companion Dog title, and the advantage of showing an unpopular obedience breed is that everyone thinks you're brave even for trying!

In fact, you may end up with a top ten obedience dog for your breed if it is especially unpopular, just for completing the Novice title!

All obedience titles require three "legs" (qualifying scores) at three different trials. To earn a qualifying score, each exercise must be passed and a minimum 170 out of 200 possible points must be earned. The order is as follows:

1. Dogs compete first in Novice obedience. The prescribed exercises require the dog to heel on and off lead, stand while a stranger examines it, come when called, and stay with a group of other dogs—in short, those things that every companion dog should know. Not surprisingly, the title earned is the Companion Dog (CD) title.

2. At the next level, Open, more off-lead exercises are required, plus jumping, retrieving, and out-of-view stays. Three Open legs earn a Companion Dog Excellent (CDX) title.

3. The most difficult level, Utility, adds the requirements of hand signal exercises and scent discrimination. Receiving three qualifying scores earns the coveted Utility Dog (UD) title. If a dog earns ten additional Utility legs, it becomes a Utility Dog Excellent (UDX), and if it earns first or second placements in Open or Utility classes, it earns points toward the 100 points needed to become an elite Obedience Trial Champion (OTCH).

*Junior showmanship competition can reach international levels, with extremely skilled competitors. (English setter).*

Note that noncompetitive titles, such as the CD, CDX, UD, and UDX, are placed behind a dog's name, while the competitive OTCH title is placed before a dog's name. Before setting your sights on an OTCH, contact the AKC and ask for the Obedience and Tracking Regulations.

Contact a local obedience club, or attend a show, obedience trial, or tracking test and talk to local competitors who seem to have happy working dogs. Different obedience instructors have very different ideas about how to train dogs, and you need to find a group with which you feel comfortable.

You may fear that obedience training your dog will sap it of its showmanship. Poor, military, rough training might just do that, but gentle training will only build confidence and reliability in your show dog. So much of what we ask our show dogs to do requires a high level of happy obedience, and a good obedience trainer strives for a

*Obedience competition captures the spirit of the human-dog relationship. (Golden retriever)*

happy attitude just as much as a the trainer of a conformation dog.

If you compete in Obedience, remember that Companion Dog means just that. Getting angry at your dog because it failed a trial defeats the purpose of obedience as a way of encouraging the human-dog bond. Besides, if your dog fails an exercise, more than likely, it was your fault!

## The Right Track

If you prefer the great outdoors, and especially enjoy quiet misty mornings alone with your dog, then *tracking* may be the sport for you.

Some dogs have an innate tendency to trail, but all breeds can be taught to use their noses and track. A Tracking Dog (TD) title is earned by following a human trail about 500 yards long that was laid up to two hours earlier. A Tracking Dog

Excellent (TDX) title is earned by following an older and longer trail having more turns, with more obstacles and distractions along the way. The highest title of Variable Surface Tracker (VST) requires that a dog follow a trail over a variety of terrain, including urban streets or even inside a building.

It can be difficult to find fellow tracking enthusiasts, but start with your local obedience club. Peruse catalogs and find any local dogs with tracking titles, then contact their owners. If this fails to get results, obtain one of the several books available on tracking and follow their training instructions. Start by requesting the Obedience and Tracking Regulations from the AKC.

## Jack Be Nimble...

Undeniably one of the most exciting competitions for dogs, handlers, and spectators, competitive *agility* has taken the dog world by storm. With different height categories, agility is open to any breed, although some breeds are admittedly more agile than others. Dogs fly through a course of obstacles that may include a tunnel, narrow bridge, seesaw, jumps, and a pause on command. There are Novice, Open, and Excellent classes, and the AKC awards, in increasing level of difficulty, the titles Novice Agility Dog (NAD), Open Agility Dog (OAD), Agility Dog Excellent (ADE), and Master Agility Excellent (MAX).

Agility trials are also sponsored by the United States Dog Agility Association (USDAA), the original governing body for the sport in the United States. Contact your local obedience club, kennel club, or the AKC or USDAA in order to find a group with which to train (see Useful Addresses and Literature, page 139).

## Outstanding in the Field

Hunting breeds can prove their mettle in hunting tests and field trials. Different events are held for different breeds, or groups of breeds, depending upon the type of hunting for which the breeds were developed.

- Beagles, basset hounds, and dachshunds are judged on their ability to trail a rabbit. Competitions are divided into braces or packs of different sizes.
- Pointing breeds (Brittanys, English setters, German shorthaired pointers, German wirehaired pointers, pointers, Gordon setters, Irish setters, viszlas, weimaraners, and wirehaired pointing griffons) are run in pairs and are judged on their ability to find, point, and retrieve birds.
- Retrievers (Chesapeake Bay, curley-coated, flat-coated, golden, and Labrador retrievers, and Irish water spaniels) are required to remember the location of downed birds, and then retrieve them to their handlers.

- Spaniels (clumber, cocker, English cocker, English springer, field, Sussex, and Welsh springer) are required to seek, flush, and retrieve birds on both land and water.

Field Champion (FC) and Amateur Field Champion (AFC) titles are both extremely prestigious and competitive titles, perhaps comparable only to an obedience championship in difficulty. But just as in obedience, in most breeds your dog can earn noncompetitive titles, such as Junior Hunter (JH), Senior Hunter (SH), or Master Hunter (MH) by demonstrating its hunting ability as scored against a set of minimal requirements. Contact the AKC and request the regulations for your particular breed.

*The most exciting competition for both spectators and competitors is agility. (Cardigan Welsh corgi)*

## Get Along, Little Doggy!

Herding breeds (as well as rottweilers and samoyeds) are eligible to compete in *herding* tests and trials. Dogs demonstrate their ability to herd sheep, goats, cattle, or ducks under their handler's direction. Contact your national breed club for more information, or contact the AKC and request the herding regulations.

# The Allure of Coursing

The sighthound breeds (Afghan hounds, basenjis, borzois, greyhounds, Ibizan hounds, Irish wolfhounds, pharaoh hounds, Rhodesian ridgebacks, salukis, Scottish deerhounds, and whippets) are eligible to compete in *lure-coursing*, in which they chase an artificial lure in a zigzag pattern around an open field. Dogs are

*Coursing dogs compete in brightly colored "blankets," and may also wear protective leg wraps. (Greyhound)*

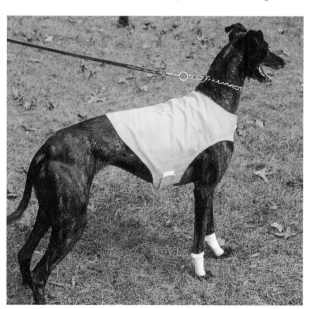

judged on speed, agility, endurance, enthusiasm, and follow (some dogs cheat and meet the lure head on!). Contact the AKC or the American Sighthound Field Association (ASFA) for a lure-coursing rule book and list of clubs in your area. The AKC awards the noncompetitive Junior Courser (JC) and Senior Courser (SC) suffix titles, as well as the competitive Field Champion (FC) prefix title. The ASFA holds more trials, and awards the competitive Field Champion (FCH) title as a suffix, as well as ongoing levels of the prestigious Lure Courser of Merit (LCM) for continued wins in the Field Champion stake.

# Rats!

Breeds that originated to "go to ground," that is, go underground into dens or tunnels in pursuit of small quarry, can compete in *earth-dog* tests, in which dogs must enter an artificial tunnel and bark or scratch at caged rats or artificial quarry. Eligible breeds are dachshunds and the following terriers: Australian, Bedlington, border, Cairn, Dandie Dinmont, smooth and wire fox, Lakeland, Norfolk, Norwich, Scottish, Sealyham, Skye, Welsh, and West Highland white. Contact the AKC or your national breed club for the names of earthdog enthusiasts in your area. You may also try contacting one of the Jack Russell Terrier clubs, which sponsor their own "go-to-ground" meets and are more likely to have a training session open to all breeds in your region. Request the earth-dog regulations from the AKC.

# Barking up the Right Tree

Both the AKC and the UKC provide an extensive list of activities for coonhound breeds (treeing walkers, black and tans, plotts, English, bluetick, and redbone). Events include night hunts, field trials, and bench shows. Interestingly, only the black and tan coonhound can be shown at regular AKC conformation events. For more information, contact the UKC or the AKC coonhound department.

# Jack of All Trades

The best dogs are multi-talented, and the prestigious *Schutzhund* titles require dogs to pass tests in tracking, obedience, and protection. Although most breeds are eligible to compete, the sport is dominated by Doberman pinschers, rottweilers, Bouvier des Flandres,

Belgian tervurens, Belgian malinois, giant schnauzers, and especially, German shepherd dogs. Three levels of competition are available, with the titles of Schutzhund I, II, and III awarded. Other advanced titles in tracking, drafting, and obedience are also awarded. Contact one of the Schutzhund clubs for a complete set of rules.

*One of the most versatile of breeds, German shepherd dogs compete for titles in conformation, obedience, agility, tracking, herding, and Schutzhund.*

## Chapter Ten
# Show Business

There really is no business like show business—for all the businesses you'll be supporting! Just in case you are dismayed that the only things you can spend money on are a new dog, wardrobe, grooming equipment, motel fees, gasoline, and entries, here are some additional spending opportunities.

*Pack carefully— you may not have time to shop for necessities when you get there.*

## Taking the Show on the Road

If you have only one or two small dogs, and plan to attend only local shows, you are either very lucky or very smart. Just put them into a small cage in the back seat and away you go! But somewhere along the way most people acquire a few more dogs and journey to more distant shows and accumulate more "stuff" that must accompany them. Vans and minivans are the most popular dog show vehicles. Cages are needed and they should be secured in place. Handy accessories include an awning for shade and cover when grooming or when the dogs are in the X-pen, and an X-pen carrier for the front of the vehicle. If you can afford to go all out, a generator and roof air-conditioner are wonderful, especially for southern shows.

### Motels

Most people stay in motels when attending out of town shows, but motels that allow dogs, even show dogs, are becoming more and more scarce. Dog show exhibitors have let their dogs bark incessantly while left unattended in rooms and allowed them to rip up carpeting, and urinate and defecate on the carpets. They groom the dogs in the rooms leaving clumps of hair stuck to everything and clogging the bathtub and sink. Some walk their dogs on the motel lawns and do not clean up after them. Exhibitors leaving their rooms in such disarray can be reported to the show-giving club and ultimately be suspended from the AKC. Their behavior endangers the future of our sport, because if there's no place to stay, who will go to the dog show?

*You may think the object of going to the dog show was to win a ribbon, but your dog knows the object is to go shopping at all the booths!*

## Camping

The alternative is to camp out at the show, and owners who travel with a lot of dogs usually find it is more convenient to buy a motor home so that they don't have to leave any dogs at home. Dog show exhibitors spend the night in everything from vans to castles on wheels, as well as an occasional tent. Camping usually involves some sacrifices, but there is peace of mind in knowing where you will spend the night, and besides, you're right at the show first thing in the morning!

Camping etiquette entails giving your neighbors adequate room for their awning and X-pens, not parking your generator next to their pens or front door, not letting your dogs bark incessantly, and, if possible, not running your generator all night. Clamp a trash bag on the side of your X-pen and clean up all dog waste immediately, place it in the bag, and change bags often. Keep a shallow pan of water and deodorizer in which to place the scoops should they become soiled. Maintain good housekeeping habits and leave your site just as you found it.

## Air Travel

Eventually you may find yourself eyeing a show on the other side of

*Shows are a good places to find unusual dog care items and colorful accessories.*

the continent. Other people fly their dogs to shows. Should you? It depends. In most cases dogs fly with no problem, but flying is not without danger. If you could not live with yourself if something happened to your dog because you wanted it to be at a show, then don't fly. Many people have made this decision.

Small dogs are at an advantage when flying to shows, if they can fit in a cage that can be placed under the seat. Contact the airline and find out the necessary dimensions for the cage. Make reservations early, as the number of canine passengers allowed in the passenger compartment is usually limited.

**Overheating:** Most dogs that have been lost during flying have succumbed to overheating. The baggage compartment is pressurized and heated, but not air-conditioned. If the plane sits on the runway for a long time in hot weather, the compartment can overheat, similar to leaving the dog in a parked car. In addition, dogs have been loaded onto the wrong flight, traveled to the wrong destination, and sat unclaimed until they were tracked down. If you must fly your dog, be a nuisance. Ask that you be notified when it is loaded. Fly only at night in the warmer months. Don't give sedatives before flying; although it may seem like a good idea, they interfere with the dog's ability to cool itself and can do more harm than good. Brachycephalic breeds are the most chancy to fly, and generally should not be flown at all in the summer unless they can fly in the passenger cabin.

**Feeding and bedding:** Don't feed your dog before a long flight, and put soft but disposable bedding in the bottom of the cage. Fill a clip-on water bucket and freeze it the night before so the dog will have water during the flight that otherwise would have been spilled during loading. A giant chewbone that has no chance of being swallowed may help occupy your jet-setter.

# Showcasing Your Dog

Let's face it—as satisfying as it is to do well with your dog, it's even better when everyone else knows

about it. It's like that tree falling in the forest question: If a dog wins at a show and nobody knows, does it really win? A plethora of dog magazines are out there just waiting for your advertising dollar. The forum you choose will depend upon your advertising budget and the people you want to reach.

## Magazines

In general, as a newcomer you will want to first advertise in a magazine devoted only to your breed. The readers will be more interested in your dog, and such magazines are usually full of ads from both big time winners as well as dogs that may have won nothing. Single-breed magazines are kept through-out the years by dedicated breeders; they document the ongoing history of a breed. Decades from now, breeders may be looking through such a magazine and spot your ad and say, "I've always wondered how that dog looked..."

At the other end of the spectrum are the slick all-color all-breed magazines. Because they are sent to the judges free of charge, dogs that are being heavily campaigned are spotlighted in these ads in hopes of influencing judges. Unless you are specialing your dog, your money will be wasted in such a magazine.

Before whipping up an ad, read a couple of issues first. Remember that you are advertising to your competitors; don't make the mistake of claiming that your dog is better than that motley bunch of mutts they're showing. Don't mention the names of dogs you have beaten in your ad. Most important of all, don't publish anything but the best picture of your dog. If you don't have a good photo, don't take out an ad.

## Why Advertise?

Does advertising influence judges? Any judge would say no. But face recognition can be a factor (if only subconscious) in convincing a judge that your dog is the one to beat. An unsure judge can perhaps gain confidence in the knowledge that other judges have also liked your dog. But magazines are chock full of ads, and to be effective you must undertake a long-term advertising campaign, something economically out of reach for most people. Within the classes, advertising will not have any effect on judges' decisions. Judges are inundated with free dog magazines and are unlikely to pay any attention to most of the dogs advertised.

If you plan to become part of the established dog world, you will need to advertise, at least in your breed magazine. Not only are the ads great for showing your neighbors, but other breeders may develop an interest in using your dog at stud, or in purchasing a relative. Perhaps most important, if you show or breed your dog, you owe it to your breed to help document the breed's history.

## Chapter Eleven

# The Secret of Success

## Every Dog Has Its Day

**S**urely the expression "every dog has its day" came from a dog show. Eventually, the worst dog of your breed ever created will win over far more deserving dogs, including yours. Perhaps the judge was impressed by some rare attribute this dog possessed, or perhaps the judge was insane or incompetent.

All dogs have shortcomings, including whatever dog beat your dog. It is human nature to focus on those shortcomings in other people's dogs, and to forgive them in your own. In truth, in most classes there is no obvious one and only possible ranking of dogs. There may be an obvious winner, or an obvious loser, or there may not be, but if the same class is judged by five different judges, you may very well get five different rankings. The point is, although you may often think your dog was unjustly treated, the judge may have actually made a reasonable decision.

This is not to say judges are infallible. Some judges, simply put, are incompetent. Others are dis-

honest. And even good honest judges make mistakes.

Losing with a beloved dog—your pride and joy—hurts your feelings and dashes your hopes. As you leave the ring you may experience a mixture of disappointment, anger, and humiliation. Your friends will tell you the judge was blind. You will agree, immediately pointing out the faults of the winning dog. At this point the hardest thing to do is to shut up. But do it. Watch the rest of the judging. Go back to your car and

*Win or lose, remember— it's just one person's opinion. (West Highland white terrier)*

*Part of a winning attitude is the absolute belief that your dog is the best and will surely win. (Vizsla)*

take your dog for a walk. Don't say a word about the judging or the winning dogs. Give yourself a cooling off period. Then if you want to say nasty things, save them for your most intimate friends. Don't say anything you will regret. Don't blame the winners for winning, even if they didn't deserve to. It's not their fault the judge made a mistake.

Have you ever watched the Miss America pageant and not agreed with the final choice? Sometimes the choice seems utterly incomprehensible and so it is at dog shows.

You've read the standard. You've studied movement. You position yourself so you can scrutinize movement from every direction. The most cowhocked and wobbly elbowed dog in the ring places first. How can this be?

First, remember that soundness is only part of the equation. Some judges put a great deal of emphasis on down-and-back movement; some consider it only a formality. It

goes back to the old type versus soundness controversy. Perhaps this judge favored type, or side movement, and perhaps this dog was very good in those areas.

No, you say, he was no better than the others. But what about what you couldn't see from ringside? In coated breeds you can't feel that a dog has a shallow chest, or no muscle tone. And you surely can't spot missing teeth or an overshot bite from 20 feet away. The judge has better than a ringside view of every exhibit; perhaps this is the explanation.

No, you say, you had the opportunity to personally go over each exhibit, and no such flaws were evident. Judges make thousands of decisions each day, placing class after class in order. Sometimes they just plain slip up.

No, you say, no one could make such a mistake. Maybe, then, you have discovered that at times, dog shows can be as unfair as the rest of life.

## Judges: It Takes All Kinds!

Judges are human; they have personality flaws. When these flaws include self-doubt, greed, or dishonesty, everyone suffers. One wonders why people would want to call themselves judges of dogs if they can't, or won't, judge dogs. Bear in mind that the ranks of judges come from the ranks of exhibitors, and they include all kinds.

Some judges are knowledgeable, honest, and hardworking. They know that their decisions are taken seriously, and they appreciate the effort that each and every exhibitor has made to bring their dogs to them. They judge dogs, not people, and they do it well. These are the judges who have become legends, the ones under whom everyone wants to boast a win.

Some judges, though honest and hardworking, are not as knowledgeable as they should be in all breeds. Insecure in their own opinions, they look for clues about which dog might really be the best. Clues include showmanship, grooming perfection, and especially, a familiar and respected face on the other end of the lead. It is my belief that in most such cases the search for clues is subconscious; the judge really does believe the dog that walks in with the well-known handler is the quality in the ring.

Some judges have everything but confidence in themselves; they don't have the courage to really judge dogs. I am always reminded of the tale of the emperor's new clothes, in which a conniving tailor convinces all in the realm that only those with high morals can see the garments he has made for the emperor. The citizens watch the naked emperor parade by in his "new clothes" and declare them beautiful! Experienced handlers with clever advertising can similarly convince a timid judge that any knowledgeable judge would recognize their dogs' hidden attributes.

Some judges are knowledgeable and hardworking, but not honest. Some can't resist putting up a friend, and you, as a newcomer, are not likely to be that friend. The handlers or long-time exhibitors they see in show after show are. They are also more likely to give a win to someone who can return the favor, often another judge who happens to be playing exhibitor that day, or the show chairman for another kennel club, who might just be inclined to have such a kindly judge hired for their upcoming show.

Remember, too, that you might just be wrong. Judges have studied dogs for many more years than you have, and they may be influenced by subtleties that you have not yet recognized, or they may be able to see through handling ploys that have you fooled. Beware of kennel blindness, the inability to see faults in one's own dogs. (Be just as wary

*Some judges emphasize movement . . . (Keeshond)*

*Some judges emphasize type . . . (Shiba inu)*

of kennel "X-ray vision," the tendency of some newcomers to pick their own dogs apart, probably so that no one else will think they're too kennel blind to see its faults!)

I always utter the following old saying to myself when I think my dog has been unjustly overlooked: "Pearls before swine." It's not my fault or my dog's fault that the judge was not blessed with either taste, intelligence, or integrity. Somehow that expression seems to make me feel better. Then I look at the winners; sometimes I see that there was good reason that they beat us, and sometimes I can't see it for the life of me.

We all have judges we love to hate. For a long time mine was a judge who put an unsound class dog with a nice head over my perfect moving special with the less than perfect head profile. "They don't run on their heads," I grumbled. For years I avoided and condemned this demon judge. Then, as luck would have it, there he was judging my breed at a very important show. Did I stay away? No! I was showing a different dog, one known for his beautiful head. Rather than hold a grudge, I remembered what this judge considered to be so important. I entered and won. Always try to understand why you win or lose. You may not always be showing the same dog.

The question you will be tempted to ask the judge is "What didn't you like about my dogs?" Unless you are sincerely interested in the answer, don't ask. Most people want to ask this so they can then dispute that their dog has that trait, or argue that it is not important. Most judges reply with something like, "It's not that I didn't like your dog, I just liked the others better." This, of course, tells you nothing. If you really want to learn about your dog, ask the judge if you could talk later, with your dog with you, and have the judge critique your dog. Again, make this request only if you really want the truth.

Every dog has its day. Maybe tomorrow will be your dog's day. Don't you hope your fellow exhibitors will be happy for you?

# You Win Some...

A dog show is a giant process of elimination; only one dog leaves the show undefeated at the end of the day. Technically speaking, all of the others are losers. You and your dog will leave the show defeated almost every time you show. But don't leave a loser.

- **Set realistic goals.** Dog show exhibitors are gamblers by nature. They prove this by the very fact that they enter under unknown judges against unknown dogs and have every confidence that they will win! And in those weeks between sending in the entries and arriving at the show, a lot of daydreaming can occur. Not only will the judge recognize the gleaming qualities of your wonder dog and give it the major, but he will also be so taken with it that he will award it BOB over that special that really doesn't deserve to be doing all that winning. And then that group judge has always been good for you—she's bound to give you a piece of the group, maybe even first. At that point, it's a one out of seven chance of going BIS! Now how happy do you think you will be when you go to the real show and win WD for a point? You should be happy, but if you've let your fantasies take over your reason, you will likely be sorely disappointed instead. Dreaming of wins is fine, but don't confuse dreams with reality and don't let your inability to live up to dreams spoil your reality.
- **Determine what it will take to make you happy.** Different people are satisfied with different levels of achievement. As you show more and more, you should start to win more and more, but at the same time you become less satisfied that you haven't won at the next level of competition. Unfortunately, each successive level is a little harder to reach than the last, so everyone is certain to be stuck at certain plateaus of achievement at some time.
- **Try to avoid getting into "can't win even if you win" situations.** Such situations arise when, even if you do win, you won't be particularly thrilled, and you have very little chance of doing better at that show. For example, if you have a champion otterhound, and you are entered in a show and find there is only one other otterhound entered (and you happen to know it's a six-month-old puppy), and the group judge only puts up handlers, don't go. If you win BOB you won't be satisfied, and if you lose BOB you

*Showing a fine animal to its best advantage is its own reward. Winning is a bonus. (Australian shepherd)*

SALUKI CLUB OF AMERICA

NATIONAL SPECIALTY

**BEST BRACE**

LEXINGTON, KY.　　JUNE 1992

*Class wins at specialties can be very rewarding, and most specialties also offer several non-regular classes. The Brace class is for two matched dogs.*

really won't be happy, and there's very little chance of doing anything in the group. Unless you can go to the show for other reasons than winning, it will not be a rewarding experience.

• **Try another strategy.** If you are unhappy with the way your luck is going at shows, maybe it's time to reevaluate how you are picking shows and why you are setting the goals you have. If your aim is to have a champion as soon as possible, then you will want to enter every show that comes along. If your aim is to be a top breeder, you will want to do the same. Such an approach often has the disadvantage that a very good dog may not get a chance to win at more prestigious shows, or to get the exposure at larger events. If your aim is to win or place in a

group, you may want to find the smallest show in your area, preferably one held the same weekend as a large prestigious show that would attract most of the big winners. If your goal is to have a top ten winner, you will have to make the commitment to go to as many shows as possible and to travel in order to find the most advantageous judges.

If you don't have a lot of dogs waiting in line to finish, and don't want to get into the specialing rat race, why be in such a hurry to finish a dog? Some people have only a couple of dogs that they try to finish at "quality" events, usually specialties, supported shows, or prestigious all-breed shows. This approach has the disadvantage that the chances of winning are quite low; however, in many cases even a class win at such an event can be more rewarding than points at just any old show. Since the chances of winning are small, the emphasis tends to be on meeting other exhibitors, socializing, exchanging ideas, and studying the dogs.

• **Try another field.** If you feel that you're stuck at an unsatisfactory level in the show ring, why not take a vacation from it and try obedience or agility or field work for a while? Become involved with the national breed club or local clubs, or with breed rescue or local humane organizations. Combine other interests. If you are a hobby photographer, set out to make a photo record of all the dogs in your breed, or put together a breed calendar. Submit photos to dog magazines or book publishers. Are you a writer? Write about your experiences and send them to a dog magazine. Do your interests run to more scientific questions? Get involved with breed genetic research. Computers? Start or become part of a home page or bulletin board for your breed on the Internet. Develop a computer pedigree file for your breed. All of these activities will ultimately help your breed more, and be more rewarding, than would collecting a fistful of blue ribbons.

- **Winning isn't everything.** That phrase has been repeated until everyone is sick of hearing it, but it really is true. Since most dog exhibitors will lose many more times than they win, if they depend on winning to be happy, then they'd better count on being sad. But besides the competition, what else is there at dog shows? Two very important things: dogs and people.

- **Enjoy your dogs as dogs.** Make every trip to a show an adventure for your dog. Schedule stops at state parks along the way or at other nature areas that both you and your dog can enjoy. Bring your camera so you can have a journal of your travels with your dog and make your dog show trips a special time shared between the two of you.

- **Make friends.** This seems trite and obvious, but somehow many exhibitors have the idea that they can't compete without hating their competitors. They can't stand to see them win, and resent any good fortune that may go their way. It's as though there were a limited amount of happiness in the world, and that if someone else gets some of it, there will be less for you. Needless to say, not only do these people have very few friends (then who could they complain about?) but they are usually very unhappy after every dog show because they couldn't prevent everyone else from winning something.

  Not only is the chance to socialize with friends a major motivation for going to shows, but through them you have yet another chance of winning (and you don't even have to pay the

*The best handlers take both winning and losing in stride. (Pekingese)*

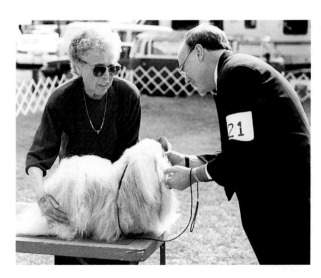

*Dogs don't know if they win or lose. They just want to have a grand outing with their loved ones. Don't spoil their time just because you may be disappointed. (Yorkshire terriers)*

entry fee). Think about it. If you only care whether or not *you* win, you will likely be very disappointed, but if you are good friends with one of your competitors, you can bask in their win as well (well, almost as well) as your own—and now it's as though you had two chances to win! This has been my greatest "secret" to getting satisfaction from dog shows. I like a good many of my competitors, enough to root for their dogs and to be genuinely pleased at their successes. And in a few cases I've found myself in a "can't lose" situation, in that I was in a ring full of people, all of whom I would be sincerely pleased to see win.

- **Root for the breed winner in the group.** Hoot and holler and clap and urge your breed representative on to the win. I once

decided to do this for a dog I didn't particularly care about, and found it was so much fun when he won the group I felt like I had really shared in the win!

- **Relax.** Winning isn't everything, and when you realize that, you just may do a better job handling and win more. The surest way to lose a show is to approach it with an "I *must* win this show" attitude. Don't make ultimatums: "If we don't win a major this weekend, I'm going to quit showing him." You can almost guarantee a loss like that.

When I showed my first special, we lost every single time. We lost and lost, and I kept getting more and more tense, and finally set an ultimatum and quit showing him. I ran him in field trials and trained him in obedience, and then decided, since we were to be at the show for an obedience trial anyway, to enter BOB competition as well. Naturally, the obedience ring and the conformation ring were at the opposite ends of a large show hall, and naturally, we were scheduled to be in both rings at the same time. We must have run five miles back and forth seeing which ring he had to be in first. Obedience turned out to be first, and he passed his individual exercises, but the group stays were scheduled at the exact same time as his conformation. I offered to skip conformation, but the kindly obedience judge demanded we go to our breed ring and that they would all wait for us. Oh, no! I didn't really want to show and lose again that badly, and I was much more concerned about getting his first leg in obedience. But we ran to the other end of the building, went into the breed ring out of breath and totally preoccupied with the obedience ring, and (to my shock) won BOB over a good entry. And then he even passed his stays! The most important thing that happened that day, though, was that I realized that it was my attitude that was causing us to lose. So I forced myself to be more causal about winning and losing, and to set other goals, such as, "Let's just have fun and maybe look good to the spectators." We started winning, enough to win over 60 more BOBs and to be in the top ten for two years!

**Remember:** It's really not that important. Somehow, certain events and accomplishments loom as great lifetime achievements, but they really mean very little in the scheme of things. We tend to attach a great deal of significance to goals we have not yet attained, but upon reaching them we find that we were really the only ones that cared about them. Can you name the top ten dogs in your breed from two years ago? Probably not. But every dog in there had an owner who put a great deal of effort into getting it into the top ten, and who was extremely proud of the accomplishment; everyone else has forgotten.

*Winning will never change the true worth of your dog in its most important role— companion. (Shar pei)*

Winning and losing are not the important aspects of dog owning. Enjoying your dog and ensuring that both of you lead happy lives is. Don't let winning interfere with happiness; when it does, it's time for a change.

If you want to know how to be miserable at a dog show, heed this advice: Set your goals high, go there to win, snub your competition, and approach each show as though it will be your last. And if that's not enough, you can kick your dog when you lose.

## It's a Dog Eat Dog World

"My dog's better than your dog" went the typical challenge among neighborhood kids. And so goes the attitude among most dog show exhibitors. Of course we love our dogs and think they're the best but adults should behave with more tact than children. They should, but many don't.

*This handler's intense attention to his dog conveys the message to the judge that his is the best dog in the ring. (Weimeraner)*

Unfortunately, many dog show exhibitors use their dogs to say, "I'm better than you are." This results in incredible rudeness and lack of consideration at dog shows.

The next time you feel like stroking your own ego, stop for a second and consider whether your listener could really be interested in what you are telling them or whether you are telling it at their expense. Think before you tell someone who has just lost to you that the judge "just told me that my dog was the first decent representative of the breed he's seen in months" or to give a 20-minute monologue on every win your dog has had in the last six months. It is certainly justifiable to boast of a big win of which you are proud (and your first point win can be even more exciting than

someone else's tenth group win), but unless you're with people who really care, it's boorish to dominate the conversation with a blow-by-blow description of every reserve your dog won and what each judge thought of your dog.

## Mind Your Manners

For people who are never short on compliments for their own dogs, or perhaps relatives of their own dogs, many dog fanciers have virtually no compliments for anybody else's dogs. It's as if they have a limited supply of compliments and they need to spend them all on themselves. You might listen to these people tout their great dog for half an hour, and even though your dog may be at your side, it apparently put on an invisible cloak beforehand because no compliments will come its way. You can't expect everybody to do flips over your dog, but surely it wouldn't kill these people to choke out a "Pretty color" or "What a cute personality" or "You can tell he really loves you" or any such noncommittal compliment somewhere between the "Perfect front" and "Classic expression" they are using to extol their own dog's virtues.

## Accepting Compliments

At the same time, it is important to accept compliments graciously, not with, "Well, of course, all of my dogs have this correct movement that you just never see in other people's dogs. No offense, but I just can't see how today's judge put your dog's son over him. That judge can't see movement. And did you notice my dog's ear set? Perfect..." Perhaps it was responses like this that made people stop giving compliments in the first place. I'll never forget the time when I complimented a well-known breeder on one of her dogs, and her reply was simply, "How would *you* know?"

*A dog with a good attitude not only looks its best, but is fun to show. (Afghan hound)*

Because dog showing involves a lot of emotional highs and lows, it is sometimes difficult to be a gracious loser or winner. Just the same, be careful not to denigrate wins that you or others may have had. It may seem "cool" to crumple that specialty reserve ribbon in disdain, or to curse your terrible misfortune at only getting second in group, but remember that many people would give their eye teeth for those wins. How must it make them feel about their wins (or losses) that day? And please, when somebody wins, keep your opinions about the judge's lack of expertise to yourself. I can't count the number of times I've been excited over a big win only to have somebody tell me afterward what a "crazy old loon" that judge is, and "you wouldn't believe the awful dogs she put up at the last show." Why on earth would somebody feel the need to make such a comment? Would it really be so bad to let the winner enjoy the win? Similarly, a word of congratulations or a few claps of the hands really would not kill most people, even though they may not be ecstatic about the win-

ner. It's a long group ring when you must trot in dead silence, with the only sound your own footsteps. Yet there are your fellow breed exhibitors, sitting with stony faces and quiet hands, so jealous of the winner they can't bear to be polite.

Don't blame someone because they won. Isn't that why you entered? Unless they cheated (which is hard to do), if you don't like the winner, then blame the judge, not the winner.

Some people may have learned to be gracious losers, but have a hard time being gracious winners. As difficult as it may have been for a loser to say, "Congratulations," it is inexcusable for the winner not to reply with a simple "Thank you." Although perhaps well-meaning, it is inappropriate to comment that "It was nothing, the judge really had no choice. Who else could he have gone with? This judge is probably the world authority on the breed, you know," or "It's just BOB, big deal." It would be much more polite to say, "Thank you, this really means a lot to

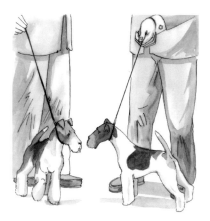

*Allowing terriers to face off, or "spar," shows off the dog's conformation as well as fearless temperament, but can be misinterpreted by spectators who think the dogs are being encouraged to fight.*

me" or, if it was a close decision, "Thank you, but it was obviously a close race between our two dogs," or even, "Yes, it seemed as if this judge preferred this style of dog today." If someone has been thoughtful enough to congratulate you, don't make them regret doing so with an inconsiderate reply.

### Snobs

Dog people can not only be inconsiderate and rude, they can also be incredible snobs. Such snobbery can be based on any number of real or imagined attributes, including the wins of one's dogs, number of dogs owned, years of activity in the breed, type of motor home driven, or any other stupid reason that comes to mind. Many times snobbery is encouraged by others giving their respect merely because someone is wealthy or has had a breed for a long time. Of course, years of experience should count for something, but it depends on what you do with

those years. Someone who studies diligently by reading, watching and asking can learn more in a year than others might in ten years.

The number of dogs owned is a similar sort of thing—you can learn a lot more about dogs with more dogs, but not if they're sitting out in the kennel. Someone with just a few dogs who takes the time to interact with them in many different ways can acquire a wealth of knowledge. While on the subject, a wealth of dollars does not indicate a wealth of knowledge. Hiring handlers to choose new prospects and handle the big winners may deprive wealthier owners of important learning experiences. The less wealthy do-it-yourselfer who has to learn about every aspect of showing from the bottom up is more likely to acquire an in-depth knowledge of dogs. Wealthy exhibitors usually can afford to amass more dogs, titles, and wins than can their poor counterparts, and such accomplishments add to the illusion that they must really know about dogs.

More than anything, dog fanciers tend to let their ownership of champions and big winners go to their head. And who wouldn't be proud of their multi BIS, BISS American Canadian Mexican Champion? In none of these titles is there a clause reading that the owners of said-titled dog are thereafter elevated to champion status themselves, and thus better than the owners of non-champions. But far too many people seem to interpret it that way. Titles do reflect hard work, quality dogs, some knowledge, and a lot of luck. Luck not only in showing, but even in the selection of a puppy. If a breeder picks out two puppies for two novice buyers, and one turns out well and finishes but the other doesn't, does that make the owner of the champion any more knowledgeable than the owner of the non-champion? Yet it happens. How on earth can somebody be judged inferior because their dog's shoulders are straight? How can a person possibly be equated with the quality of the dog they own?

I've heard exhibitors put down another because that exhibitor continued to show a dog that was clearly not a winner, but that dog was her pet. She loved it and enjoyed showing it despite the fact that she realized it had faults. How could she be faulted for being faithful to her dog and participating in a sport? Winning is only one of many reasons to attend dog shows, but with rude and ruthless behavior, fewer people will choose to participate simply for their love of dogs.

## In the Public Eye

One day you will be the person that a newcomer will look to as his or her dog show representative. Try to remember how people treated you when you went to *your* first show, and try to do better!

Experienced dog handlers do a number of things that the average family, attending their first dog

show, may misinterpret. Many of the behaviors we encourage in our show dogs are those that most people discourage in their pets. Forging ahead on the lead, begging for bait, and jumping up on the handler are all traits that most pet owners are told are not acceptable. The dog show world must eventually consider how they appear to the public if they wish to encourage new participants.

- Many handlers use their mouth as an extra hand, storing liver in it, baiting the dog, and then replacing the liver. Yuk! Every onlooker I've ever seen who saw this for the first time has been nauseated. Such practice does nothing to enhance a respectable image of the sport. Use a pocket or a bait pouch.

*You and your dog are ambassadors fro the breed and the world of dog showing. Your good example and good advice are vital to the future of the sport. (Siberian husky)*

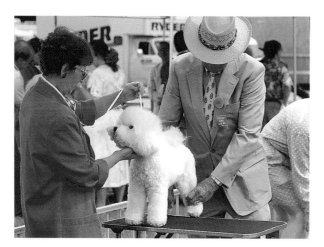

*Bichons are always examined by the judge on a table. Here the dog is being carefully examined by the judge in the show ring.*

- Many breeds are commonly picked up by their head and tail so that the coat is not messed up when putting the dog on the table. Although it doesn't hurt the dog, families who have spent hours teaching their children not to pull the dog's tail have often been upset to see this. If you use the head and tail method, do so subtly and as gently as possible.
- Some terrier breeds are sparred (see page 130) in the ring. The object of sparring is to get the dogs on their toes, demonstrating their self-confidence and showing off their conformation to best advantage. The object is not to let them fight, or even to lunge at each other. Such actions give the public the idea that dog fighting may be next on the agenda.
- No matter how upset you are with judging or your dog, be a model of good sportsmanship.

Treat your dog and fellow exhibitors with courtesy and respect. Think of yourself as an ambassador for your breed and for dog shows in general.

- Take the time to talk to the confused family attending their first dog show. Explain why dogs are being sparred, or that it doesn't hurt lightweight dogs to be picked up briefly by their head and tail. Point them to the judging schedule so they can find their favorite breed. Explain the basics of judging. If you don't have time to talk, tell them why, deliver them to someone who can talk to them, or promise to get back to them after you show, and then actually live up to that promise. Who knows, perhaps in another 20 years that person will become an exhibitor, and then a judge, because of your encouragement, and maybe they'll just give you a Best in Show!

## You Are the Future

There are many ways to give back to the sport of dogs. By supporting breed rescue and research, educating the public, encouraging newcomers, and setting a fine example by breeding with the utmost restraint and responsibility as well as by loving your dogs first as pets and second as show animals, you will achieve more than you would by simply amassing a room full trophies. Of course, the goal is to have it all!

# Know the Lingo

## General and Showing Terms

**Baiting** Use of tidbits, usually boiled liver, to get a dog's attention.

**Balance** Overall proportion and symmetry of conformation.

**Best** Short for Best in Show.

**Bitch** Female dog.

**Bloom** Healthy condition.

**Brace** Two matched dogs.

**Brood bitch class** Competition based on the quality of two or more of a dam's offspring.

**Chalking** Use of chalk or powder to whiten, clean, or harshen the texture of the coat.

**Class dog** Dog entered in any class for nonchampions.

**Coarse** Large-boned, lacking in refinement.

**Common** Lacking breed type or refinement.

**Conformation** Physical make-up.

**Cryptorchid** A male in which one (unilateral) or both (bilateral) testicles have failed to descend.

**Dog** Male dog.

**Dumped** Said of a dog that lost when it was expected to win.

**Entire** A male having two normally descended testicles.

**Fault judging** Judging that penalizes dogs' weak points, instead of rewarding their strong points.

**Finishing** Completing a dog's championship.

**Four-square** A dog that stands in such a way that a line drawn between its paws would form a square.

**Free-baiting** Using bait to guide a dog so that it poses itself.

**Futurity** Competition for puppies in which the litter must be entered ("nominated") when extremely young, or before birth.

**High in rear** A dog that is higher over its rear quarters than over its front quarters.

**High-stationed** Tall and long-legged.

**Indefinite listing privilege (ILP)** AKC registration for dogs that are clearly purebred but have no proof of breeding; an ILP number enables dogs to compete in most AKC events except conformation.

**Kennel-blindness** The inability to see faults in one's own dogs.

**Leg** Qualifying score in obedience or agility.

**Major** Win of three, four, or five points.

**Match** Informal and unofficial practice competition.

**Monorchid** A male in which a testicle has never developed;

incorrectly used to refer to a unilateral cryptorchid.

**National** Short for national specialty, the specialty sponsored by the national breed club.

**Pet quality** A dog unable to finish its championship.

**Plucking** Pulling out loose hair by hand.

**Posting** Leaning backward when posed.

**Put down** To groom and prepare for the show ring.

**Put up** To award first place.

**Racy** Long-legged with a slight build.

**Rangy** Long-bodied with a shallow chest.

**Set up** To pose a dog by hand.

**Show potential** A puppy that should mature into a show quality dog.

**Show quality** A dog that has a reasonable chance of finishing its championship.

**Showing** A dog giving a spirited performance in the ring

**Sparring** Allowing two terriers to face off and approach each other in a domineering manner.

**Special** Champion that continues to be shown in BOB competition.

**Specialing** Showing a special, usually with the goal of having that dog become one of the top dogs in that breed.

**Specialty** Show for only one breed of dog.

**Square-bodied** Height at withers equal to length from point of sternum to point of croup.

**Stacking** Posing a dog by hand.

**Standard** The official blueprint for a breed.

**Stripping** Removal of the undercoat and dead outercoat without losing the harsh texture; plucking.

**Strung up** Showing a dog on a very tight lead.

**Stud dog class** A class judged on the merits of one or more of the stud's offspring ("get").

**Substance** Fairly heavy bone and musculature.

**Supported entry** Show in which trophies are offered by a breed club; more prestigious than an average show, but less prestigious than a specialty show.

**Sweepstakes** Additional competition for dogs of select age groups held in conjunction with a specialty show.

**Team** Four matched dogs.

**Top producer** A dam that produces three or more champion offspring, or a sire that produces five or more champion offspring, in a calendar year.

**Top ten** The ten dogs of a breed that defeat the most other dogs of that same breed in either BOB, Group, and Best in Show competition (all-breed top ten) or in Best of Breed competition only (breed top ten). A dog receives one ratings point for every dog it defeats during the year.

**Typey** Displaying important essential characteristics of the breed, especially of the head.

**Variety** A subtype of a breed that is shown separately, but that can be interbred with other varieties of the same breed.

**Veteran** Older dog, usually over seven years of age.

**Weedy** Lacking sufficient bone and musculature.

**Wicket** Device for measuring the height of a dog, consisting of two vertical bars joined by a horizontal bar that can be adjusted for height.

## Coat Terms

**Corded** Coat that is intertwined in the form of long, narrow mats giving a mop-like appearance (example: komondor).

**Feather** Long hair on the ears, backs of legs, and beneath the tail.

**Flag** Long fringe on the tail.

**Jacket** Tight body coat of a terrier.

**Mane** Profuse growth of hair on the rear of the neck.

**Plume** Profusely feathered tail carried over the back.

**Ruff** Profuse growth of hair on the front of the neck, or that surrounds the entire neck.

**Stand-off coat** Coat that sticks out from the body rather than lying flat (example: Norwegian elkhound).

**Topknot** Tuft of hair on top of the head.

## Color Terms

**Belton** Intermingled colored and white hairs.

**Brindle** Irregular vertical bands of dark hair overlaid on lighter hair.

**Harlequin** Spotted coloration, used specifically for the Great Dane.

**Hound colored** Black, tan, and white, with a black saddle.

**Merle** Dark patches overlaid on a lighter background of the same pigment type; Also called dapple.

**Parti-color** Spotted.

**Piebald** Black patches on a white background.

**Sable** Black-tipped hairs in which the undercoat is of lighter color.

**Saddle** Dark patch over the back.

**Spectacles** Dark markings around the eyes.

**Ticking** Small flecks of coloring on a white background.

**Wheaten** Pale yellow color.

## Head Terms

**Apple head** Extremely domed skull.

**Brachycephalic** Broad head with short-muzzle (example: Pekingese).

**Butterfly nose** Spotted or partially unpigmented nose.

**Chiseled** Clean-cut muzzle and foreface.

**Dish-face** Nose tipped up.

**Dolichocephalic** Narrow head with long-muzzle (example: collie).

**Down-faced** Muzzle curved downward.

**Dudley nose** Liver- or flesh-colored nose.

**Fill** Fullness beneath the eyes, not chiseled.

**Flews** Upper lips, especially those that are pendulous.

**Haw** Exposed nictitating membrane (third eyelid), especially if unpigmented.

**Mesatacephalic** Medium-width head with medium-length muzzle (example: beagle).

**Occiput** Highest point at the back of the skull, above where the neck joins the head; in many breeds it forms a crest and is quite prominent.

**Stop** Transition area from back-skull to muzzle, often demarcated by an abrupt depression.

**Snipey** Weak, pointed muzzle lacking underjaw.

## Teeth Terms

**Bite** Occlusion; relationship of the upper and lower jaws when the mouth is closed.

**Full dentition** No missing teeth.

**Level bite** When upper and lower incisors meet evenly.

**Overshot bite** When upper incisors overlap lower incisors, leaving a gap between the teeth.

**Scissors bite** When upper incisors just overlap lower incisors, such that the rear surface of the upper incisors touches the outer surface of lower incisors.

**Premolars** Small teeth situated just to the rear of the fangs (canines).

**Punishing mouth** Strong, powerful jaws.

**Undershot bite** When lower incisors extend beyond upper incisors

## Ear Terms

**Button ears** Semi-prick ears in which the top portion folds forward (example: fox terrier).

**Bat ears** Large, erect ears (example: French bulldog).

**Drop ears** Long, hanging ears.

**Rose ears** Small ears folded back in repose (example: greyhound).

**Prick ears** Ears that stand upright (example: German Shepherd dog).

## Neck Terms

**Bull-neck** Thick, muscular, often short neck.

**Crest** Arched area near the top of the neck.

**Ewe neck** Neck that is arched so that the top line of the neck is concave, and the bottom is convex.

**Goose neck** Overly long, thin neck lacking strength and shape.

**Throaty neck** Neck with loose skin.

## Body Terms

**Barrel chest** Rounded ribcage.

**Brisket** Chest or sternum area.

**Cobby** Compact.

**Herring gutted** Gradual slope from a fairly shallow chest to tuck-up.

**Loin** Region between the ribcage and croup.

**Rib spring** Arch formed by the ribcage; more spring refers to more arch.

**Roach back** An overly arched, convex topline.

**Shelly** Narrow, shallow chest and body.

**Short-coupled** Short loin area.

**Slab-sided** Flat-ribbed.

**Swayback** A sunken, concave topline.

**Topline** Line formed by the withers, back, loin, and croup.

**Tuck-up** Area under the loin in a small-waisted dog.

## Forequarter Terms

**Bowed front** Forelegs that curve out between the elbows and pasterns.

**Down in pastern** Weak, overly sloping pastern.

**East-west front** When feet turn out to the sides, pointing away from each other.

**Fiddle front** East-west front combined with a bowed front, so that the assembly looks like a fiddle.

**Lay back** Angle at which the shoulder is set on the dog's body.

**Knuckled over** Steep pastern, or with a reverse slope.

**Loaded shoulders** Overly muscled or lumpy forequarters.

**Out at elbow** Elbows that stick out from the sides of the ribcage.

**Return** Set-back of the upper arm under the dog's body.

**Shoulder** Scapula; also used (incorrectly) to refer to both the scapula and upper arm (humerus) region.

**Shoulder angulation** Angle formed between the scapula and humerus.

**Toed-in front** Pigeon toed; feet pointing toward each other.

## Rearquarter Terms

**Bandy-legged** Wide, bowed-legged rear quarters.

**Cow-hocked** Viewed from behind, the point of hocks point toward each other, resulting in the rear feet pointing outward.

**Lower thigh** Area from stifle to hock, also called second thigh.

**Rear angulation** Angles formed between the pelvis, thigh bone (femur), and second or lower thigh bone (tibia/fibula).

**Sickle-hocked** Viewed from the side, an over-angulated joint between the lower thigh and hock; an inability to straighten this joint when moving.

**Well let-down** Short hocks.

## Foot Terms

**Cat foot** Short, round foot.

**Dew claws** Extra toes on the insides of the front, and sometimes, rear legs.

**Hare foot** Long, narrow foot.

**Paper foot** Flat foot.

**Splay foot** Toes that are not close together.

## Tail Terms

**Bob tail** Very short, almost stump-like tail (Example: Pembroke Welsh Corgi).

**Brush tail** Tail covered in hair in such a manner as to give it a bottle-brush appearance (Example: Siberian husky).

*"Show me!" "No, show me!" How about a brace? (Salukis)*

**Docked tail**  Tail cut to a shorter length.

**Gay tail**  Tail carried above the level of the back.

**Saber tail**  Slightly curved, low-carried tail.

**Screw tail**  Short, twisted tail.

## Movement Terms

**Close behind**  Moving with hocks close together.

**Crabbing**  Side-winding.

**Crossing-over**  When viewed from the front (or rarely, the rear), the legs converge beyond the midline.

**Drive**  Strong thrust from the hindquarters.

**Gait**  Way of moving.

**Hackney**  High-stepping front movement.

**Loose movement**  Erratic movement suggestive of poor muscle development.

**Lumbering**  Heavy, ungainly movement.

**Pacing**  Moving both legs on the same side of the body in unison, as though hobbled together.

**Pounding**  Front feet hitting the ground with a jarring reaction.

**Reach**  Length of forward stride.

**Single tracking**  As viewed from the front or rear, the legs converge toward the center line of balance as the dog trots.

**Sound**  Good movement viewed from the front and rear.

**Trotting**  Moving diagonal legs in unison.

# Abbreviations

## Awards
**AOM**  Award of Merit
**BIM**  Best in Match
**BIS**  Best in Show
**BISS**  Best in Specialty Show
**BOB**  Best of Breed
**BOS**  Best of Opposite Sex
**BOV**  Best of Variety
**BOSV**  Best of Opposite Sex Variety
**BOW**  Best of Winners
**GR1 (GR2, GR3, GR4)**  Group 1st
  (2nd, 3rd, 4th)
**RWB**  Reserve Winners Bitch
**RWD**  Reserve Winners Dog
**SBIS**  Specialty Best in Show
**WB**  Winners Bitch
**WD**  Winners Dog

## AKC Titles
**CH**  Champion
**AFC**  Amateur Field Champion
**FC**  Field Champion
**DC**  Dual Champion (CH/FC)
**CD**  Companion Dog
**CDX**  Companion Dog Excellent
**UD**  Utility Dog
**UDX**  Utility Dog Excellent

**OTCH**  Obedience Trial Champion
**TC**  Triple Champion (CH/FC/OTCH)
**TD**  Tracking Dog
**TDX**  Tracking Dog Excellent
**VST**  Variable Surface Tracking Dog
**UDVST**  Utility Dog/Variable
  Surface Tracking Dog
**UDXVST**  Utility Dog Excellent/
  Variable Surface Tracking Dog
**NA**  Novice Agility
**OA**  Open Agility
**AX**  Agility Excellent
**MX**  Master Agility
**JH**  Junior Hunter
**SH**  Senior Hunter
**MH**  Master Hunter
**JC**  Junior Courser
**SC**  Senior Courser
**HT**  Herding Tested
**PT**  Pre-trial Tested
**HS**  Herding Started
**HI**  Herding Intermediate
**HX**  Herding Excellent
**HC**  Herding Champion
**JE**  Junior Earthdog
**SE**  Senior Earthdog
**ME**  Master Earthdog

# AKC Classification of Breeds

**Sporting Group (Group One)**
Brittany
Pointer
Pointer (German Shorthaired)
Pointer (German Wirehaired)
Retriever (Chesapeake Bay)
Retriever (Curly-Coated)
Retriever (Flat-Coated)
Retriever (Golden)
Retriever (Labrador)
Setter (English)
Setter (Gordon)
Setter (Irish)
Spaniel (American Water)
Spaniel (Clumber)
Spaniel (Cocker), Black
Spaniel (Cocker), ASCOB
Spaniel (Cocker), Parti
Spaniel (Cocker English)
Spaniel (Field)
Spaniel (Irish Water)
Spaniel (Sussex)
Spaniel (Welsh Springer)
Viszla
Weimaraner
Wirehaired Pointing Griffon

**Hound Group (Group Two)**
Afghan Hound
Basenji
Basset Hound
Beagle (13″)
Beagle (15″)
Black and Tan Coonhound
Bloodhound
Borzoi
Dachshund (Longhaired)
Dachshund (Smooth)
Dachshund (Wirehaired)
Foxhound (American)
Foxhound English
Greyhound
Harrier
Ibizan Hound
Irish Wolfhound
Norwegian Elkhound
Otter Hound
Petit Basset Griffon Vendeen
Pharaoh Hound
Rhodesian Ridgeback
Saluki
Scottish Deerhound
Whippet

**Working Group (Group Three)**
Akita
Alaskan Malamute
Bernese Mountain Dog
Boxer
Bullmastiff
Doberman Pinscher

Giant Schnauzer
Great Dane
Great Pyrenees
Greater Swiss Mountain Dog
Komondor
Kuvasz
Mastiff
Newfoundland
Portuguese Water Dog
Rottweiler
Saint Bernard
Samoyed
Siberian Husky
Standard Schnauzer

## Terrier Group (Group Four)
Airedale Terrier
American Staffordshire Terrier
Australian Terrier
Bedlington Terrier
Border Terrier
Bull Terrier (Colored)
Bull Terrier (White)
Cairn Terrier
Dandie Dinmont Terrier
Fox Terrier (Smooth)
Fox Terrier (Wire)
Irish Terrier
Kerry Blue Terrier
Lakeland Terrier
Standard Manchester Terrier
Miniature Bull Terrier
Miniature Schnauzer
Norfolk Terrier
Norwich Terrier
Scottish Terrier
Sealyham Terrier
Skye Terrier
Soft Coated Wheaten Terrier
Staffordshire Bull Terrier
Welsh Terrier
West Highland White Terrier

## Toy Group (Group Five)
Affenpinscher
Brussels Griffon
Cavalier King Charles Spaniel
Chihuahua (Long-Coated)
Chihuahua (Smooth-Coated)
Chinese Crested
English Toy Spaniel (Blenheim and
    Prince Charles)
English Toy Spaniel (King Charles
    and Ruby)
Italian Greyhound
Japanese Chin
Maltese
Manchester Terrier (Toy)
Miniature Pinscher
Papillon

*The real winners are those who share an unconditional love with their pet. (Newfoundland)*

Pekingese
Pomeranian
Poodle (Toy)
Pug
Shih Tzu
Silky Terrier
Yorkshire Terrier

## Non-Sporting Group (Group Six)

American Eskimo Dog
Bichon Frise
Boston Terrier
Bulldog
Chinese Shar-Pei
Chow Chow
Dalmatian
Finnish Spitz
French Bulldog
Keeshond
Lhasa Apso
Poodle (Miniature)
Poodle (Standard)
Schipperke

Shiba Inu
Tibetan Spaniel
Tibetan Terrier

## Herding Group (Group Seven)

Australian Cattle Dog
Australian Shepherd
Bearded Collie
Belgian Malinois
Belgian Sheepdog
Belgian Tervuren
Border Collie
Bouvier Des Flandres
Briard
Collie (Rough)
Collie (Smooth)
German Shepherd Dog
Old English Sheepdog
Puli
Shetland Sheepdog
Welsh Corgi (Cardigan)
Welsh Corgi (Pembroke)

# Useful Addresses and Literature

## Clubs

Owner Handler Association of
   America, Inc.
Mrs. Mildred Mesh
6 Michaels Lane (c)
Old Brookville, New York 11545

American Kennel Club
51 Madison Avenue
New York, New York 10010
(212) 696-8200: Main switchboard
(212) 696-8281: Event records and
   results
(212) 696-8276: Obedience and
   tracking
(212) 696-8388: Herding,
   Lure-coursing, Agility, and
   Earthdog
(212) 696-8238: Coonhounds
(919) 233-9767: *AKC Gazette*
   subscription, books, and videos

AKC Registration Matters:
American Kennel Club
5580 Centerview Drive
Raleigh, North Carolina 27606
(919) 233-9767

States Kennel Club
P.O. Box 389
Hattiesburg, Mississippi
   39403-0389

United Kennel Club
100 East Kilgore Road
Kalamazoo, Michigan 49001

Fédération Cynologique
   Internationale
12 rue Leopold 11
14B-6530
Thuin, Belgium

Canadian Kennel Club
89 Skyway Avenue
Etobicoke, Ontario M9W 6R4
Canada

Federación Canofila Mexicana
Apartado Postal 22-535
CP 14000
Mexico DF

Bahamas Kennel Club
P.O. Box N-9870
Nassau, Bahamas

United Schutzhund Clubs of America
c/o Paul Meloy
3704 Lemay Ferry Road
St. Louis, Missouri 63125

American Herding Breed Association
c/o Linda C. Rorem
1548 Victoria Road
Pacifica, California 94044

Hunting Retriever Club
100 East Kilgore Road
Kalamazoo, Michigan 49001

North America Hunting Retriever
    Association
P.O. Box 154
Swanton, Vermont 05488

American Sighthound Field
    Association
c/o Vicki Clarke
2234 Walnut Avenue
McKinleyville, California 95521

American Working Terrier
    Association
c/o Frank Doig
P.O. Box QQ
East Quogue, New York 11942

United States Dog Agility
    Association
P.O. Box 850955
Richardson, Texas 75085-0955

## AKC Dog Show Superintendents

Antypas, W.
P.O. Box 7131
Pasadena, California 91109
(818) 796-3869

Bradshaw, J.
P.O. Box 7303
Los Angeles, California 90022
(213) 727-0136

Brown, M.
P.O. Box 494665
Redding, California 96049
(916) 243-0775

Brown, N.
P.O. Box 2566
Spokane, Washington 99220
(509) 924-1089

Campbell, J.
P.O. Box 3070 MPP
Kamloops, British Columbia
Canada 62C 6B7

Crowe, T.
P.O. Box 22107
Greensboro, North Carolina 27420
(910) 379-9352

Houser, H.
P.O. Box 420
Quakertown, Pennsylvania 18951
(215) 376-4939

McNulty, E.
1745 Route 78
P.O. Box 175
Java Center, New York 14082
(716) 457-3371

Matthews, A.
P.O. Box 86130
Portland, Oregon 97286-0130
(503) 233-4241

Onofrio, J.
P.O. Box 25764
Oklahoma City, Oklahoma 73125
(405) 427-8181

Peters, B.
P.O. Box 579
Wake Forest, North Carolina 27588
(919) 556-9516

Rau, J.
P.O. Box 6898
Reading, Pennsylvania 19610
(610) 376-1880

Reed, R.
177 Telegraph Road
Suite 405
Bellingham, Washington 98226
(206) 738-8827

Roberts, L.
P.O. Box 4658
Federal Way, Washington 98063
(206) 952-8059

Rogers, K.
P.O. Box 230
Hattiesburg, Mississippi 39403
(610) 583-1110

Sleeper, K.
P.O. Box 828
Auburn, Indiana 46706-0828
(219) 925-0525

Wilson, N.
8307 East Camelback Road
Scottsdale, Arizona 85251
(602) 949-5389

Saldivar, E.
4343 1/2 Burns Avenue
Los Angeles, California 90029
(213) 663-5868

## Periodicals

### General
*AKC Gazette* and *Show Awards*
51 Madison Avenue
New York, New York 10010
(919) 233-9767

*Bloodlines* (UKC)
100 E. Kilgore Road
Kalamazoo, Michigan 49001-5598

*Dogs in Canada*
43 Railside Road
Don Mills, Ontario
Canada, M3A 3L9

*Dog World*
29 North Wacker Drive
Chicago, Illinois 60606-3298

*Dog Fancy*
P.O. Box 53264
Boulder, Colorado 80322

### Coonhounds
*American Cooner*
P.O. Box 211
Sesser, Illinois 62884

## Herding

*National Stockdog Magazine*
P.O. Box 402
3597 CR 75
Butler, Indiana 46721

*The Ranchdog Trainer*
Rt 1, Box 21
Koshkong, Missouri 65692

## Hunting

*American Field*
American Field Publishing Company
222 West Adams Street
Chicago, Illinois 60606

*Hunting Retriever*
100 E. Kilgore Road
Kalamazoo, Michigan 49001-5598

*Retriever Field Trial News*
4213 S. Howell Avenue
Milwaukee, Wisconsin 53207

## Obedience

*Front and Finish*
H & S Publications
P.O. Box 333
Galesburg, Illinois 61402

*Off Lead*
100 Bouck Street
Rome, New York 13440

## Schutzhund

*Dog Sports Magazine*
DSM Publishing
940 Tyler Street, Studio 17
Benecia, California 94510-2916

*DVG America*
P.O. Box 160399
Miami, Florida 33116

*Shutzhund USA*
3704 Lemay Ferry Road
St. Louis, Missouri 63125

## Coursing

*Field Advisory News*
2234 Walnut Avenue
McKinleyville, California 95521

*Open Field Coursing Newsletter*
Susan Loop-Stanley
P.O. Box 68
Glenrock, Wyoming 82637

## Terriers

*Down to Earth*
P.O. Box QQ
East Quoque, New York 11942

# Index